SLIGHTLY
OUT OF FOCUS

ROBERT CAPA

SLIGHTLY
OUT OF FOCUS

FOREWORD BY
CORNELL CAPA

INTRODUCTION BY
RICHARD WHELAN

THE MODERN LIBRARY

NEW YORK

1999 Modern Library Edition

Introduction and biographical note copyright © 1999 by Richard Whelan
Copyright © 1999 by Cornell Capa
All Robert Capa photographs copyright © 1999 by Cornell Capa
Copyright © 1947 by Henry Holt and Company, Inc.

This work was originally published in 1947 by Henry Holt and Company, Inc.
This edition published by arrangement with Cornell Capa.

The Modern Library wishes to thank the staff of Magnum Photos—and in
particular Eelco Wolf, David Strettell, and Jessica Murray—for their
invaluable assistance in assembling the Robert Capa images collected herein. Magnum
Photos, the international photographers' cooperative cofounded by Robert Capa in 1947, is
the exclusive agent for Capa's photographs.

Two books of Robert Capa's work, *Robert Capa: Photographs*
and *Heart of Spain: Robert Capa's Photographs of the Spanish Civil War*,
are currently available from Aperture Foundation,
20 East 23rd Street, New York, NY 10010.

LIBRARY OF CONGRESS CATALOGING-IN-PUBLICATION DATA
Capa, Robert, 1913–1954.
Slightly out of focus / Robert Capa: foreword by Cornell Capa:
introduction by Richard Whelan.
p.   cm.
ISBN 0-679-60328-X (alk. paper)
1. Capa, Robert, 1913–1954.   2. World War, 1939–1945—Photography.
3. War photographers—United States—Biography.   I. Title.
D810.P4C34   1999
779′.994054—dc21   99-24637

Modern Library website address: www.modernlibrary.com

Printed in the United States of America on acid-free paper

2 4 6 8 9 7 5 3

Preceding pages: NEAR TROINA, SICILY, AUGUST 4–5, 1943. *American troops
march toward the strategic hilltop town. The Germans were holding it as a
delaying action until most of their forces could be evacuated from the island.
The town controlled the main road to Messina, from which the German army
was being ferried to the Italian mainland.*

ROBERT CAPA

Robert Capa photographed five wars: the Spanish Civil War (1936–39), Chinese resistance to the Japanese invasion (which he covered in 1938), the European theater of World War II (1941– 45), the first Arab-Israeli War (1948), and the French Indochina War (1954). No one has ever photographed war with greater bravery or with more intense compassion.

He was born Endre Friedmann, in Budapest, on October 22, 1913, to middle-class Jewish parents who had a fashionable dressmaking business. His brother, Kornel, who would become a photographer under the name Cornell Capa, was born in 1918.

In May 1931, when Endre was seventeen, he was arrested for his leftist student activities against the proto-fascist regime of Admiral Miklós Horthy and was jailed overnight. The next day—thanks to the influence of the chief of police's wife, a good customer—Endre's father got him released on the condition that he leave the country after his upcoming high school final examinations. In July he departed for Berlin, where he enrolled that fall in the Hochschule für Politik to study journalism, not photojournalism. The worldwide economic depression soon made his parents unable to continue paying for his education. Forced to leave school, he naturally turned to

fellow Hungarians in Berlin for employment. He landed a job as errand boy for the outstanding photojournalistic agency Dephot and was quickly promoted to darkroom assistant, then to apprentice photographer.

In November 1932 the agency sent him to Copenhagen to photograph exiled Leon Trotsky giving a lecture to Danish students. The published story was a great success, but before the photographer could capitalize on it, he had to flee Germany, in March 1933, soon after Hitler's assumption of dictatorial powers. Endre obtained official permission to return home to Budapest, and from there he went to Paris that fall. In the cafés of Montparnasse he soon met and became friendly with fellow photographers André Kertész, David Seymour ("Chim"), and Henri Cartier-Bresson.

In the fall of 1934 André (as he then called himself) met Gerda Pohorylle, a German Jewish refugee; they soon fell in love and began living together. She typed his captions and got a job with the agency that represented him; he in turn taught her how to use a camera.

In the spring of 1936, faced with a dire scarcity of sales, André and Gerda decided to invent a glamorous and successful American photographer named Robert Capa. When Gerda made her rounds of editorial offices, she would claim that André's photographs were Capa's—and that she was doing the editors a tremendous favor by giving them an opportunity to buy the work of this elusive genius. Suitably impressed, editors bought the photographs and published them.

The name "Capa" seems to have been derived from that of Frank Capra, the Hollywood director whose masterpiece, *It Happened One Night*, with Claudette Colbert and Clark Gable, had not only won the Academy Award for the best picture of 1934 but had also won Oscars for its director and its two stars. "Robert" also came from the movies, from the actor Robert Taylor, who in 1936 was starring as Greta Garbo's screen lover in *Camille*. At the same time, Gerda changed her surname to Taro, borrowed from the young Japanese artist Taro Okamoto then living in Paris.

Soon, the mysterious Capa really was quite famous. When the ruse was discovered, André realized that he would have to assume the name Robert Capa and live up to the reputation of this imaginary sensation.

In August 1936 the twenty-two-year-old Capa began his thorough and passionate coverage of the Spanish Civil War. It was on his first trip that he made his famous photograph of a Spanish Loyalist militiaman beginning to collapse after having been fatally shot. The picture was published internationally to great acclaim.

Gerda Taro, who often worked with Capa in Spain but who was also becoming an independent photojournalist, remained in Madrid in July 1937 when Capa returned to Paris to take care of some business. Caught in a confused retreat while she was covering the fighting at Brunete, west of Madrid, Taro was crushed to death by a Loyalist tank. Capa, who had hoped to marry her, never fully recovered from his grief.

Reluctant to return to the war that had killed his lover, Capa spent six months of 1938 in China with Dutch filmmaker Joris Ivens, documenting resistance to the Japanese invasion that had begun the previous year. Because Japan was allied with Germany, the war in China was widely viewed as the eastern front of the international antifascist struggle, of which Spain was the western front.

That fall Capa returned to Spain to cover the departure of the International Brigades, and he went on to photograph the battles of Mora de Ebro and the Río Segre, both on the Aragon front. In December the prestigious British magazine *Picture Post* published eight pages of battle photographs by the twenty-five-year-old Capa and proclaimed him "The Greatest War-Photographer in the World."

—

Soon after the end of World War II, Capa and his friends Henri Cartier-Bresson, Chim, George Rodger, and William Vandivert founded Magnum, a cooperative photo agency. For the rest of his life, Capa would devote much of his time to guiding the operations of the Magnum offices in Paris and New York. His greatest enthusiasm was for the young photographers whom he invited to join the agency. He considered them his extended family, and he worked hard to get assignments for them, encouraged them, advised them, lent them money, and took them out to dinners and parties. Although he had become an American citizen in 1946, Capa lived in Paris during the late forties and early fifties. There he enjoyed a glamorous life of afternoons at the racetracks, evenings at nightclubs with beautiful women, and all-night poker games with such friends as John Huston and Gene Kelly.

During the late forties Capa collaborated on several projects with literary friends. In the summer of 1947 he spent a month traveling in the Soviet Union with John Steinbeck; the book they produced, *A Russian Journal,* juxtaposed Steinbeck's text with Capa's pictures. The following year *Holiday* magazine sent Capa and journalist Theodore H. White to Hungary and Poland. And in 1949 he and novelist Irwin Shaw produced the book *Report on Israel.*

In April 1954 Capa spent three weeks in Japan as the guest of the publishing firm Mainichi Shimbun to help launch a new photography magazine. In Tokyo, Osaka, Kyoto, and elsewhere he concentrated on photographing children. While in Japan, he accepted an assignment from *Life* to spend a month in Indochina to fill in for a photographer who had to return to the States. On May 25, Capa accompanied a French convoy on a mission to evacuate two indefensible forts in the Red River delta. When the convoy halted, Capa went into the field beside the road to photograph a group of French soldiers. There he stepped on an antipersonnel mine and was killed.

For a memorial portfolio of Capa's work published in *Popular Photography,* John Steinbeck wrote, "Capa knew what to look for and what to do with it when he found it. He knew, for example, that you cannot photograph war, because it is largely an emotion. But he did photograph that emotion by shooting beside it. He could show the horror of a whole people in the face of a child. His camera caught and held emotion.

"Capa's work is itself the picture of a great heart and an overwhelming compassion. No one can take his place. No one can take the place of any fine artist, but we are fortunate to have in his pictures the quality of the man.

"I worked and traveled with Capa a great deal. He may have had closer friends but he had none who loved him more. It was his pleasure to seem casual and careless about his work. He was not. His pictures are not accidents. The emotion in them did not come by chance. He could photograph motion and gaiety and heartbreak. He could photograph thought. He captured a world, and it was Capa's world."

And at a memorial service for Capa, Edward Steichen rose and said, "He understood life. He lived life intensely. He gave richly of what he had to give to life.... [He] lived valiantly, vigorously, with a rare integrity."

—RICHARD WHELAN

FOREWORD

BY CORNELL CAPA

My brother, Robert Capa, gave himself the assignment to report on man's self-created inferno, war. His compassion was for all sufferers in war, and his photographs transformed into eternal moments not only crucial events but also individual ordeals.

The travails of the decades he witnessed were tragic, but what gave him strength were his sense of humor and a self-deprecating attitude toward his own courage. These were the essential ingredients of the man, in his life and in his work. In *Slightly Out of Focus* he wrote of his experiences on D-Day:

> The war correspondent has his stake—his life—in his own hands, and he can put it on this horse or on that horse, or he can put it back in his pocket at the very last minute. I am a gambler. I decided to go in with Company E in the first wave.

In making that decision he was following the advice he often gave to his fellow photographers: "If your pictures aren't good enough, you're not close enough." But behind the humor and the irony and bravery lay great sensitivity, which led him to remark, with characteristic understatement: "It's not easy always to stand aside and be unable to do anything except to record the sufferings around one."

Robert Capa's life is a testament to difficulty overcome, a challenge met, a gamble won except at the end, when he stepped on a land mine in Indochina and his role as witness was terminated. Born without means to travel, with a language not useful beyond the borders of a small country, Hungary, he managed to experience the world through a universal means of communication, photography. He was thus able to speak to us all, then and now.

During his short time on earth he lived and loved a great deal. He was born without money, and he died the same. What he left behind is the story of his unique voyage and a visual testimony affirming his own faith in humankind's capacity to endure and occasionally to overcome.

NEW YORK CITY
April 1999

CORNELL CAPA, Robert's younger brother, had a distinguished career as a photojournalist for *Life* magazine and for Magnum Photos. In 1974 Cornell Capa founded the International Center of Photography in New York City. He served as its director until his retirement, in 1994, and is now its Founding Director Emeritus.

INTRODUCTION

BY RICHARD WHELAN

The precocious Budapest teenager who would eventually become known to the world as Robert Capa did not aspire to be a photographer. He wanted to be a writer—a reporter and a novelist. It was by chance, not by choice, that he drifted, or was pushed by circumstances, into photography.

Even while his unprecedentedly powerful photographs of war—in Spain, in China, and throughout the European theater of World War II—were establishing him at the summit of photojournalism, Capa never abandoned his dream of being a writer first and a photographer second. It was, therefore, with great satisfaction that he saw, in 1947—on the dust-jacket flap of *Slightly Out of Focus,* though not on its title page—the first appearance of his favorite credit line: "By Robert Capa, with photographs by the author." That credit would subsequently appear above his debonairly amusing articles for *Holiday* magazine about skiing in the Alps, about partying and gambling at such glittering resorts as Deauville and Biarritz, and about his travels and adventures in countries ranging from Norway to Hungary.

—

Since most copies of the original edition of *Slightly Out of Focus* now lack their dust jackets, most readers plunge into Capa's text unaware of his disclaimer that appeared on the front jacket flap. "Writing the truth being obviously so difficult," he stated, "I have in the interests of it allowed myself to go sometimes slightly beyond and slightly this side of it. All events and persons in this book are accidental and have something to do with the truth."

Such a disclaimer was necessary for the simple reason that Capa wrote his book not to stand as a historical document but rather to serve, with little alteration, as the basis for an entertaining screenplay. Most of the stories in the book were perfectly true, but Capa disguised the names of some of the principal characters, speeded up the sequence of some events, and changed a few minor details. For example, in the second sentence of the first chapter Capa states that his studio apartment was "on the top floor of a small three-story building on Ninth Street." It was, in fact, on the top floor of a five-story brownstone at 60 West Ninth Street. We must assume that Capa thought that a three-story building would conform more closely than a five-story one would to the Hollywood notion of a picturesque Greenwich Village structure.

Capa was a born storyteller, and there were few things that he enjoyed more than cheering up a friend or a stranger with a hilarious account of one of his picaresque adventures. When the literal truth mattered, he told the literal truth. But when no one but a pedantic bore would insist upon that, Capa saw absolutely no reason to restrain himself from a bit of embroidery to make a good story even better—which is to say, more amusing, usually at his own expense.

Recently Capa's reputation has been cleared of the most serious allegation ever made against his honesty in an instance that mattered very much. An elderly British journalist, whose memory was no longer reliable, charged that Capa had made his famous photograph of a collapsing Spanish Loyalist militiaman during training exercises rather than during a battle. But Capa had been far away from where the journalist claimed, and a Spanish historian has confirmed that the man in the photograph—whom both he and the man's family identified as Federico Borrell García—was fatally shot at the

time and place of Capa's picture: near the village of Cerro Muriano, a few miles north of Córdoba, on September 5, 1936.

———

The voyage of which Capa gives an account in the opening chapter of *Slightly Out of Focus* was not his first experience of a transatlantic convoy to Britain. He had made a similar crossing in the spring of 1941 to join his friend Diana Forbes-Robertson (whom he had first met in Spain) to collaborate on a book, entitled *The Battle of Waterloo Road,* about how the Cockney residents of a neighborhood in London's East End were surviving the blitz. Dinah, as her friends all called her, was a daughter of the great actor Sir Johnston Forbes-Robertson and was the wife of the then famous journalist Vincent ("Jimmy") Sheean, whose memoir, *Personal History,* had been a best-seller. Dinah's sister was Lady Maxine Forbes-Robertson, whose nickname, Blossom, became "Flower" in *Slightly Out of Focus.* Blossom's second marriage, in 1932, was to F. G. (Frederick George) Miles, who then owned a flying school. An enthusiastic and knowl-edgeable aviator, Blossom soon began to work with her husband on designing a plane that was to be known as the Hawk. It was an instant success, for it was faster, more comfortable, and less expensive than its principal rival, the Haviland Moth. Wartime contracts poured in, and by the early 1940s Miles Aircraft, with a large factory in Reading, was employing six thousand workers.

Dinah and Jimmy took Capa along on numerous weekend visits to the Mileses during the summer of 1941, and they all became very friendly. Because Capa had renewed his friendship with Blossom and Miles soon after his return to London in 1942, it was quite natural for him to drop in on them in mid-February 1943, on his way back to London from an assignment.

Among the house guests that weekend was John Justin, a very handsome, slender, half-English, half-Argentinean actor who had starred as Ahmad, the deposed ruler, in Alexander Korda's wonder-ful 1940 film, *The Thief of Bagdad;* after that he had temporarily given up his movie career to become a pilot in the RAF. With Justin was his glamorous twenty-five-year-old wife, Elaine, a ravishing beauty with a most alluring figure, a very feminine and sexy demeanor, and a gorgeous head of pale strawberry-blond hair that led Capa to nickname her "Pinky." Her marriage with Justin was already on the rocks, but they had been unable to get a divorce. As Pinky later recalled, she and Capa "took one look at each other and knew that something was starting." In *Slightly Out of Focus* the story of their romance is woven around and through Capa's account of his coverage of the war.

———

In the end Pinky did, in fact, marry Chuck Romine, whose privacy Capa protected under the name Chris Scott. With Pinky lost to him and with the war in Europe over, a few weeks passed during which the photographer may well have felt (as he complained in both the first and the last sentence of his book) that there was "absolutely no reason to get up in the mornings any more." But he soon had a very good reason indeed to get up: a romance with Ingrid Bergman, who was in Europe to entertain American troops.

Before she went home, she and Capa made plans for him to follow her to Hollywood, as he did in December 1945. He was hardly a stranger in town, for during the war he had become friends with directors John Huston, George Stevens, William Wyler, Irving Reis, Anatole Litvak, and Billy Wilder. Litvak soon jokingly complained, "After only two weeks here, Capa is getting invited to parties it took me ten years to get invited to."

In January 1946, William Goetz, head of International Pictures, hired Capa as a writer and apprentice director-producer for the ample but hardly extravagant salary of four hundred dollars a week. He was to write his war memoirs as the basis for a screenplay (he had begun writing autobiographical short stories in Sun Valley, Idaho, in 1941, at which time Ernest Hemingway had helped him polish up the first few), and he was to spend time on the sets, in the cutting room, and at screenings of classic films. But he found he couldn't concentrate on his writing, and he was thoroughly bored by his other responsibilities.

Most frustrating of all, he was able to see very little of Bergman, for not only her jealous husband (Dr. Petter Lindstrom, from whom she was eager to get a divorce) but also the ubiquitous columnists

watched her closely. It wasn't until Hitchcock began filming *Notorious,* starring Bergman and Cary Grant, that Capa had any excuse for hanging around her.

When Bergman raised the question of marriage, Capa told her that, since he saw no future for himself in Hollywood, he was going to have to get back into photojournalism and couldn't tie himself down; if they were married, he wouldn't feel free to accept the dangerous assignments that were his specialty. Nor could Bergman possibly accompany him on his travels. She told all this to Hitchcock, who served as her father confessor, and he would eventually incorporate their dilemma into his film *Rear Window,* in which Jimmy Stewart plays a photojournalist fending off (surely more harshly than Capa would have done) marriage hints from the high-fashion arbiter played by Grace Kelly.

———

In mid-June 1946, while he was on a visit to New York, Capa signed a contract with publisher Henry Holt for his war memoirs, which were beginning to come along, although the stipulated delivery date of August 15 of that year was totally unrealistic. Capa then went back to Hollywood to see whether he and Bergman could save their romance without marriage. No longer working for International Pictures, Capa was supposed to devote himself to writing. Instead, he spent his days photographing on the set of Bergman's new film, *Arch of Triumph,* and his evenings partying at the studio with Bergman and a lively group of friends.

Later in the summer, while watching his friend Charles Korvin rehearse for his role in a movie entitled *Temptation,* Capa said that he could play the Egyptian servant Hamza better than the Egyptian who had been hired for the part. The character, his face largely hidden by the hood of his burnoose, spent most of his brief appearances on camera bowing and backing out of the set, and he spoke a few lines of gibberish. Irving Pichel, the director, decided that Capa's accent sounded right and fired the real Egyptian.

That was the end of Capa's Hollywood career—and of his affair with Bergman. He was soon on his way to Turkey to direct a documentary film for the *March of Time.* The experience was not pleasant, at least partly because he had to work hard every night to finish his book. The manuscript was almost four months late, and the publisher was furious. In Ankara, through the U.S. Information Service, Capa hired an English-speaking graduate student, Rosette Avigdor, to type as he dictated, a procedure that explains some of the book's direct, conversational quality. He sent the last chapter off to Holt just before Christmas 1946. Working together, Capa and Avigdor became such good friends that when she told him she would be leaving for New York in January to study at Columbia University, he suggested that she move in with his mother. Both women liked the idea, and Avigdor became Capa's "Turkish sister."

———

When *Slightly Out of Focus* was published, in the spring of 1947, the reviews were mostly excellent. The *New Republic*'s critic wrote, "Violating all war-correspondent traditions, Capa has told what happened to him—within the framework of a tenderly uproarious love story...gay, swift, entertaining." The *New York Herald Tribune Book Review* praised the "running narratives of private and professional life—not like any other story of the war and yet revelatory footnotes to every other book that has been written." The highest praise was, of course, reserved for Capa's photographs. The *Philadelphia Inquirer* declared, "What Tolstoy does with words for Sevastopol, Hemingway for Caporetto, Crane for the Civil War, Capa achieves with his camera."

The most eloquent tribute of all, however, came from a young Pulitzer Prize winner named John Hersey, with whom Capa had struck up a warm friendship in Sicily in 1943. In an article about Capa entitled "The Man Who Invented Himself," published in the short-lived magazine *47*, Hersey wrote, "Despite all his inventions and postures, Capa has, somewhere at his center, a reality. This is his talent—which is compounded of humaneness, courage, taste, a romantic flair, a callous attitude toward mere technique, an instinct for what is appropriate, and an ability to relax. At the very core, he even has modesty. He has the intuition of a gambler.... [He] has humor. He has a clear idea of what makes a great picture: 'It is a cut of the

whole event,' he says, 'which will show more of the real truth of the affair to someone who was not there than the whole scene.'

"Above all—and this is what shows in his pictures—Capa, who has spent so much energy on inventions for his own person, has deep, human sympathy for men and women trapped in reality."

BROOKLYN, N.Y.
April 1999

RICHARD WHELAN, an independent cultural historian, is the author of *Robert Capa: A Biography.* Together with Cornell Capa, he has edited several books of Robert Capa's photographs. His other books range from *Drawing the Line* (a political history of the Korean War) to a biography of Alfred Stieglitz.

CONTENTS

SLIGHTLY
OUT OF FOCUS

I

There was absolutely no reason to get up in the mornings any more. My studio was on the top floor of a small three-story building on Ninth Street, with a skylight all over the roof, a big bed in the corner, and a telephone on the floor. No other furniture—not even a clock. The light woke me up. I didn't know what time it was, and I wasn't especially interested. My cash was reduced to a nickel. I wasn't going to move until the phone rang and someone suggested something like lunch, a job, or at least a loan. The phone refused to ring, but my stomach was calling. I realized that any further attempt to sleep would be futile.

I rolled over and saw that the landlady had pushed three letters under the door. For the last few weeks my only mail had been from the phone and electric companies, so the mysterious third letter finally got me out of bed.

Sure enough, one of the letters was from Consolidated Edison. The second was from the Department of Justice, informing me that I, Robert Capa, formerly Hungarian, at present nothing definite, was hereby classified as a potential enemy alien, and as such had to give up my cameras, binoculars, and firearms, and that I would have to apply for a special permit for any trip that would take me more than ten miles from New York. The third letter was from the editor of *Collier's* magazine. He said that *Collier's*, after pondering over my scrapbook for two months, was suddenly convinced that I was a great war photographer, and would be very pleased to have me do a special assignment; that a reservation had been obtained for me on a boat leaving for England in forty-eight hours; and that enclosed was a check for $1,500 as an advance.

Here was an interesting problem. If I'd had a typewriter and sufficient character, I would have written back to *Collier's*, telling them that I was an enemy alien, that I could not go even to New Jersey, let alone England, and that the only place I could take my cameras was the Enemy Aliens' Property Board down at City Hall.

I had no typewriter, but I had a nickel in my pocket. I decided to flip it. If it came up heads, I would try to get away with murder and go to England; if it came up tails, I would return the check and explain the situation to *Collier's*.

I flipped the nickel, and it was—tails!

Then I realized that there was no future in a nickel, that I was going to keep—and cash—the check, and that somehow I would get to England.

———

The subway accepted the nickel. The bank accepted the check. I had breakfast at Janssen's, next to the bank—a big breakfast that came to $2.50. That settled it. I couldn't very well go back to *Collier's* with $1,497.50, and *Collier's* was definitely in for trouble.

I reread their letter and made sure that my boat was leaving in about forty-eight hours. Then I reread the letter from the Department of Justice, and tried to figure out where to start. All I needed was a release from my draft board, an exit and re-entry permit from the U.S. State and Justice Departments, a British visa, and some sort of passport to put the visa on. I couldn't afford to collect a "no" at the very beginning, so I needed an understanding ear. I was in trouble. Well, the United States was just starting to realize what trouble meant, but the British had been at war for over two years and must have got used to trouble. I decided to go to the British first.

From Janssen's to the airline terminal was a five-minute walk. I learned that there was a plane leaving for Washington in less than an hour. I bought a ticket, and *Collier's* was out still more money.

Two and a half hours later, a taxi put me down at the British Embassy in Washington, where I asked to see the press attaché. I was led into the presence of a tweedy gentleman with a very red face and a bored expression. I told him my name, but I didn't know how to start my story, so I simply gave him the two letters, the one from *Collier's,* then the one from the Department of Justice. He read the first one without showing any reaction, but when he put down the second there was a trace of a smile on his lips. Somewhat encouraged, I fished out and handed him the still unopened letter from Consolidated Edison, which I well knew was a notice that my electricity was going to be shut off. He motioned me to sit down.

When he finally spoke, he was surprisingly human. Until the war, he had been a professor of geology. The outbreak of hostilities had found him in Mexico, where he was happily studying the composition of the soil on top of tired volcanoes. He did not care much about politics, but this was war and they had drafted him as a press officer. Ever since, he had had to turn down all kinds of propositions for saving the British. He assured me that my case beat them all. I was champ! I was overwhelmed with sympathy for him, and for myself. I suggested lunch.

We went to the Carlton and had to drink many dry martinis before we could get a table. My companion warmed up considerably, and I began to feel that—along with *Collier's*—the attaché and the British Empire were going to be stuck with me, too. When we finally got a table, I picked up the menu and ordered a dozen Blue Points apiece to start. Now, five years before, in France, I had invested heavily in my drinking education, and I remembered that in every English mystery story where Lord Peter Wimsey had anything to say, oysters are washed down with that marvelous white burgundy called Montrachet. The Montrachet 1921 was at the bottom of the list, and very expensive. It was a happy choice. My companion told me that, fifteen years ago, when he had spent his honeymoon in France, he had impressed his bride with that very wine, so by the end of the bottle we were talking about our love for France—and

Montrachet. Over the second bottle we agreed that our feelings about throwing the Germans out of *la belle* France were equally strong, and after the coffee, along with the Carlos Primero brandy, I told him about my three years with the Republican Army in the Spanish Civil War, and how I had good reason to hate the fascists.

Back at the Embassy, he picked up the telephone and asked for the State Department. He got through to someone high up, called him by his first name, said that in his office was "good old Capa," that it was vitally important that I get to England, and that I would be over in fifteen minutes to pick up my exit and re-entry permits. He hung up, gave me a slip of paper with a name on it, and fifteen minutes later I was at the State Department. I was received by a precisely dressed gentleman who filled in my name and occupation on a form, signed it, and told me that all would be ready by nine in the morning at the immigration office at Staten Island, in New York Harbor. Then he accompanied me to the door, relaxed for a moment, slapped me on the back, winked, and wished me "Good luck!"

When I returned to the Embassy, my friend the attaché was a bit solemn—and worried—until I told him that my first step had been successful. This time he called the British consul general in New York. He told him that "old Capa" was leaving for England, and had absolutely everything in order, but had no passport. Ten minutes and several phone calls later, the naval attaché of the Embassy, the professor, and I were all in a little bar, drinking to the success of my trip. It was time for me to catch my plane, but before parting, the naval attaché assured me that he was going to send code messages to every port in the United Kingdom saying that I was arriving on *a* boat, with cameras and film, and that I was to be helped in every way and delivered safely to the Admiralty in London.

On the plane back to New York, I decided that the British were a great people, that they had a wonderful sense of humor, and that, when it came to the impossible, they were very nice to have around.

—

Next morning, the British consul general in New York remarked that my case was highly unusual—but that war was highly unusual too.

He gave me a very usual-looking piece of white paper, asked me to put down my name, explain why I hadn't any passport, and state my reasons for traveling.

I wrote that my name was Robert Capa; that I was born in Budapest; that Admiral von Horthy and the Hungarian government had never liked me, and that I had never liked them; that the Hungarian Consulate, since Hitler's annexation of Hungary, refused to say that I was not a Hungarian, nor would they say that I was; that, so long as Hitler was in charge of Hungary, I definitely refused to say that I was; that I was born deeply covered by Jewish grandfathers on every side; and that I hated the Nazis and felt that my pictures would be useful as propaganda against them.

I was a little worried about the spelling when I handed him back the piece of paper, but he put stamps and seals on it, a blue ribbon all around it, and—a passport was born.

———

On the morning I was to sail, there were still four or five minor permits missing. My mother, who was now living in New York, accompanied me, and while I tried to collect those last necessary scraps of stamped paper, she waited for me in the taxi. Each time I returned, she sat silently and tried to read the answers on my face. She was a very torn mother that morning, hoping for my sake that I would succeed in getting the various permits and get away; for her own motherheart, praying that something would go wrong and that I would not be able to go off to war again.

I finally had all the papers, but we were an hour and a half late for the scheduled departure of my ship, and my mother's last hope was that the boat had already left.

But when we arrived at the pier, the dirty old merchant boat was still there. A big Irish cop barred our way: I showed him my papers.

"You're late," he said. "And you'd better make it snappy."

This was as far as my mother could go. She ceased to be the representative of "brave motherhood in wartime," and was transformed into a big and loving Jewish heart. All the long-repressed reserve of tears poured out of the corners of her big, beautiful brown eyes.

The six-foot-six Irish cop put his arm around the shoulders of my little five-foot mother and said, "Lady, I'm going to buy you a drink."

I slipped a last kiss to my mother, and ran for the gangplank.

My last view of the United States was the backs of the Irish cop and my mother, crossing to the bar under the suddenly smiling skyscrapers.

II

I hurried up the gangplank. I wasn't the only late arrival. Close on the heels of two staggering sailors, I marched out of the United States.

The captain, who was standing at the head of the gangplank, turned to his mate and said, "Well, there's the last two, home to roost." Then he saw me. "And who are you?"

"I'm a rather special case, sir. I'm the traveling enemy alien."

"Well, we're carrying a strange cargo already. Suppose we go down to my cabin and see how you're listed on the manifest."

He found me duly described there, and went through my papers without comment.

"Before the war," he told me, "I carried bananas and tourists from the West Indies to England. Now, instead of bananas, I'm bringing home the bacon, and on the promenade deck I'm carrying dismantled bombers instead of tourists. Well, my boat isn't as clean as it used to be, Mr. Capa, but my tourist cabins are empty and I think you'll find your quarters comfortable."

I found my cabin and settled down. The engines were humming. After two years in the States, I was on my way back to Europe. My mind wandered back.... Two years ago, flying from France, I had arrived in this same harbor, and at that time I'd had to worry whether they would let me enter. At that time too my papers had been pure invention. I had been described as a farming expert on my way to Chile to improve the agricultural standards of that country, and had a transit visa which allowed me to stay in the States for thirty days. It had not been easy to land then...it had been difficult persuading them to let me stay...and it had needed the miracle of an English professor to let me leave....

I took out my cameras—which, since December 8, 1941, I had not even been allowed to touch—poured myself a drink, and I was a newspaperman again.

———

At dawn we anchored in Halifax harbor. Here the captain went ashore to receive instructions. Later in the day, after he had returned, I learned that we were going to cross as part of a fast convoy, that our ship would be the lead ship, and that a retired Navy captain—who was now commodore of the convoy—would command from our bridge.

I had visions of a sensational four-page spread in *Collier's,* called "Commodore of the Convoy," with dramatic photographs of this old, tottering sea dog standing on the bridge, ships sinking to fore and aft.

After dinner, the commodore sent for me. There was hardly any light on the bridge, but when I could make out his features I was disappointed. Instead of the tottering, old sea lion I had pictured, I found a trim gentleman in his fifties, and the only resemblance I could find to the character of my imagination was a pair of enormous and very bushy eyebrows. I introduced myself, and he answered that, as for himself, he was an Irishman. He immediately went on to say that he was very interested in the movie world, and found some of the Hollywood actresses rather exciting. He would have to stay on the bridge all through the trip, but why couldn't I come up every night and tell him some nice stories about Hollywood? In exchange, he would be glad to tell me everything about convoys.

The deal was quite unfair. For the commodore knew his convoys, whereas I had never been to Hollywood. But I didn't have the heart to tell him that he had mispronounced my name, that I wasn't the famous movie director, that my name was Bob Capa, and not Frank Capra at all. During the rest of the trip I would have to play Scheherazade. I could only hope that it wouldn't last a thousand and one nights!

We spent the night in the harbor. In the morning, the commodore asked me if I'd like to go along with him and visit the captains of the ships in the convoy. Most of our ships were sailing under foreign flags, and the commodore had a hard time trying to make himself understood. The Swedish and Norwegian skippers offered us aquavit and spoke rather good English. The Dutchmen had very good gin and no trouble at all. The French captain had excellent brandy, and I translated. The Greek had a murderous drink called ouzo and spoke a very fast Greek. In all, we visited twenty-three ships, and in all, we drank in twenty-three different nationalities. On the way back to our boat, the commodore complained about all the crazy foreigners and made me feel positively Anglo-Saxon.

In the afternoon we formed our convoy without difficulty. We sailed in four rows of six ships, about a thousand yards apart from each other. Our escort was kind of meager—a single destroyer and five tiny corvettes.

Our first night on the bridge, the commodore did most of the talking. During World War I he had been the captain of a destroyer, and by 1918 he was leading an entire flotilla. The names of Zeebrugge and Gallipoli floated through the air. When he finished his stories, he asked me how Lillian Gish was doing nowadays. I assured him that Miss Gish was still in excellent shape, and as we parted it looked like the beginning of a beautiful friendship.

The first four days at sea passed without excitement. I spent my days taking pictures of everything and everybody from the masthead to the engine room, and at night I was on the bridge, telling the commodore everything I could remember from the fan magazines I'd read in the waiting room at my dentist's. I hinted vaguely that I was a very discreet man, but still I let him feel that I myself may have had a somewhat active part in some of those Hollywood scandals. In exchange, he told me about the time, during one of his convoys to Murmansk, that his boots froze to the deck and how he couldn't move for three days. The commodore did not drink while on the high seas, but I had my pocket flask and fought the cold as he talked. After midnight, leaning on the rail of the bridge, I sometimes felt as if I were in a blacked-out Third Avenue bar.

So far, my "Battle of the North Atlantic" was entirely pleasant—indeed, far too pleasant. The crew, however, took a poor view of my craving for action, and was not at all upset about the possibility of the *Collier's* story being dull.

On the fifth day, we ran into a genuine North Atlantic fog. Our destroyer pulled up alongside and flashed us a message. The commodore turned to me. "If you can take pictures in a fog, Capra, you may get your damned scoop after all," he said. "A wolf pack of German submarines is laying for us about thirty miles up ahead."

Fog or no fog, the commodore decided we'd have to change our course. By now we weren't able to see the stern of our own ship from the bridge, and we were still obliged to keep strictest radio silence. Communication with the rest of the convoy had to be through foghorns. The Norwegian tanker, which had been sailing on our left, answered back with its two long and three short blasts from some-where on our right. The Greek cargo, the last ship in the convoy, some three miles behind us, blew her four long blasts somewhere fifty yards from our bow. Altogether, the twenty-three foghorns made enough noise to be heard in Berlin. The commodore cursed all Allied, neutral, and cobelligerent skippers alike. But there was no time to worry about collisions. The wolf pack had found us, and our escort was dropping depth charges.

I packed my precious passport and what was left of the *Collier's* money in my oil-silk tobacco pouch, and bitterly regretted the im-provement of my story.

The commodore gave the signal for the convoy to scatter, and from then on every ship was on its own. From time to time we heard the engines of other ships uncomfortably close, but the explosions of the depth charges grew further and further away.

Forty-eight hours later, the fog was pierced by brilliant sunshine. The twenty-three ships were all around us. Even our escort was there. In fact, we were still in formation. But the ships that had been in the middle of the convoy before were sailing on the outside; the Greek ship, which had been last, was now leading; and we ourselves were trailing in the very rear.

———

A point appeared on the horizon, and in a little while it started to signal with light flashes. Our signalman gave us the message with a perfectly straight face. "H.M.S. *Harvester* inquires, sir, whether you can spare them some beer."

"Tell them to come and get it."

The destroyer, after making one or two fancy turns around the convoy, gaily steamed up alongside. The British destroyer captain was on the bridge with a megaphone. "Surprised to see you, sir, with all your ships still floating."

"Surprised to see the British Navy floating—without beer!"

"We ran out of depth charges and had to finish off Jerry by throwing our beer barrels at them!"

———

Shortly afterwards a string of, to me, undecipherable flags was run up on our mast. The signalman translated the message for me: "Was proud to have led you from behind, but revert to original formation. Use caution."

The ships acknowledged the signal. The Norwegian tanker nearly rammed the Greek cargo; the Swedish gentleman went full speed astern and disappeared from view; the Frenchman reported that his boiler was busted and that he would have to be left behind. After four hours of milling around, the convoy proceeded with twenty-two ships.

That night, when I joined the commodore on the bridge, he ignored me for a while. Just as I was ready to go back to my cabin, he eased up. "By the way, Capra, have you ever met Clara Bow?"

———

It turned out that the destroyer had wasted its beer, for the next day the German subs were all around us again. Our destroyer put up a very photogenic smoke screen around the convoy, and radioed for help. A British destroyer patrol was due to meet us about now, and fortunately kept the appointment. As a finishing touch to *Collier's*

"Battle of the North Atlantic," we had a pretty dogfight between a German flying boat and a British Sunderland, with the entire convoy pouring black smoke from every ack-ack gun we had.

I had taken all my pictures, and my imagination had been sucked dry of stories about Hollywood, when the lighthouse in the Irish Channel came into view.

For the first time, the commodore went below, and I was left alone with his signalman on the bridge. He was a silent man and hadn't said an unnecessary word during the whole trip. He made sure that the commodore had really gone. Then he whispered to me, "The Old Man is a great chap, but—if you'll pardon my saying so—well, some of those stories he told you...!"

It made me feel a lot better, but I resolved that at the first opportunity I would send my apologies to Mrs. Frank Capra.

———

Entering the Channel, we changed formation, and the distance between ships was closed to one hundred yards. Now, for the first time, radio silence was lifted and each ship was told separately where to dock. I hoped that our ship would dock at Liverpool, and began to plan my first day at the Savoy Hotel in London. But the War Shipping Administration didn't play ball: we received orders to steam up the Irish Sea and await further instructions off Belfast.

The Savoy would have to live without me for twenty-four hours. It wasn't too bad, the commodore told me, he knew just the right pub in Belfast, and—as for him—he had a great backlog to make up!

Soon after we dropped anchor a motor launch approached, and a number of gentlemen in bowler hats from the Immigration Office boarded our ship. When it came my turn to be examined, the gentlemen concentrated busily on my documents. From time to time they shook their bowler hats and didn't appear at all satisfied. When they learned about my cameras and films, they shook their bowlers even more vigorously. I mentioned the code message from the naval attaché in Washington, but they received the news with a blank look. In desperation, I tried to be funny and said that I really wasn't Mr. Hess and that it wasn't everyone who could land in England by parachute. But they were not amused. They told me, for my information, that during the war only citizens of the United Kingdom were allowed to debark in Northern Ireland. I would just have to stay on board until we docked at some port in England proper. The authorities there could decide my fate.

The commodore seemed genuinely sorry to leave me behind. He offered me his cabin, assured me that my stories had been most interesting, and went ashore with the immigration officers. The captain, who was now in complete charge of his ship again, tried to console me by saying that in three days at the outside he would receive his orders to proceed to England. He added brightly that, inasmuch as we were not officially in port yet, the ship's stores would remain open, and that Scotch was still available at seven shillings a fifth.

I moved into the commodore's cabin, ordered a bottle of Scotch, and sat down with the First Radio to play blackjack. By ten at night, the bottle was empty, and *Collier's* was down $150. I called for another bottle, but the steward came back empty-handed, looked at me with a queer expression, and said that I was being asked for in the captain's cabin.

I stumbled up to the bridge with more than a slight feeling of impending disaster and far too much Scotch in my stomach. I made out two young naval officers with the captain. Their names were Garbidge and Miller, and after making sure that my name was Capa, they asked me to turn over my cameras, films, and notes into their custody. No, I told them, that was something I couldn't do. I was sticking with my cameras, films, and notes. What was more, I added, I was supposed to have all facilities accorded to me by the British Navy upon my arrival, and no facilities, not one, had been accorded so far. Instead, I had been rudely stranded on an empty boat out in the middle of the Irish Sea. Now I was going to stay on that boat, and when and if I ever got to England, I was going to complain bitterly.

They both mumbled something about a war being on, and retired to a corner to consult a mysterious slip of paper. After several minutes of deliberation, reading and rereading the paper at least three times, they returned, and insisted that I hand over my films, cameras, and notes without delay. This was a new tune, and I didn't like it.

Suddenly, through the Scotch mist, it all became clear to me. I offered them two to one that I could tell them what the message on the slip of paper was all about. I told them how the naval attaché in Washington was supposed to send a code message to every port in the United Kingdom, about *a* Robert Capa, arriving on *a* boat, with cameras and films, and that I and my camera and films were to be taken care of, helped through formalities, and delivered to the Admiralty in London. All they had to do now was go back and check with the Embassy in Washington and tell the Admiralty that I was on this *specific* boat, and would dock—sometime—in England.

Garbidge and Miller looked at the slip, at each other, and then handed it over to me. Sure enough, it said something about films, cameras, and Capa, but had been coded and recoded so many times that by now it was open to as many interpretations as the Bible. Garbidge, suddenly meek, asked if he could talk to me in private for a moment.

"We are sure that you are right, sir." He hesitated. "I hope you will trust us and believe what I am going to say."

I was pleased with the turn in the situation, and listened.

He explained that he and Miller were with Naval Intelligence in Belfast. Their duties the day before had been so exhausting that they went and had a drink after office hours. There they had met the skipper of a minesweeper, a schoolmate of long years before, and he had persuaded them to visit his ship, as drinks were much cheaper there than in a bar. Indeed, the drinks proved to be so cheap and so plentiful that they hadn't been able to find their office until just a little while before. That was when they discovered the message. Now, if they went back to Naval Intelligence empty-handed, they would be forced to admit the somewhat special circumstances that had delayed them. They would get into the most terrific jam if I didn't help them. If I went ashore with them, Garbidge continued, they would see to it that I got to London—cameras, films, and all—by the best and quickest way.

It was easy to be generous. I decided to help the British Navy, bought three bottles of whisky in the store to take along, and followed Garbidge and Miller. In complete darkness, we climbed down a swaying rope ladder to the smallest of motor launches—which was bobbing impatiently up and down—and pushed off.

But our troubles were far from over. The pilot turned back to my two friends and informed them that it was half past eleven at night and that Customs and Immigration were closed until eight in the morning. Under no circumstances could he put me ashore!

The three of us became extremely unhappy, but this time Miller saved the situation. "Suppose we find the minesweeper. We can spend the night there in comfort, and in the morning we'll motor over to the harbor."

———

It took us two hours to find the right minesweeper in the darkness. The skipper, after recognizing Garbidge and Miller, asked them whether they had brought any liquor back. Miller replied that they had brought not only liquor but Capa too. The skipper supposed that "Capa" might be some new drink, and invited us cordially aboard. Before any new troubles could develop, the tired pilot wisely disappeared in the darkness.

The mess room of the minesweeper barely held the four of us. The skipper inquired about the whisky and I produced my three bottles. He then inquired about Capa. Garbidge started to tell him the story, but the skipper got confused and, swaying lightly, asked, "Just tell me one thing. Is it all right or isn't it all right?"

Oh, it was definitely all right, Garbidge assured him, and anyway there wasn't anything we could do about it now.

We opened the bottles and toasted the British Navy, the merchant marine, and the minesweepers in quick succession. The skipper then turned to me and proposed a toast to King Boris, immediately adding, in a rather confidential tone, "No offense, old boy, but isn't your King Boris on the wrong side of the fence?"

I replied that King Boris didn't belong to me, that he was a Bulgarian, and definitely on the wrong side of the fence. Unfortunately, I continued, what was more of my business was that the Hungarians had Admiral von Horthy, and that he was on the wrong side too. The skipper was very sorry about that, but there were plenty of other things to toast, and we quickly changed the subject.

The next morning at six we woke up with hangovers and silent forebodings. We were just about to signal the harbor to send us a motor launch, when the chief signalman entered the cabin with a message. Orders had been received to proceed immediately to sweep mines in the Irish Sea! We signaled Naval Intelligence that Capa was going to sweep mines in the Irish Sea... that everything had an explanation....

———

Altogether we spent three days on the open sea. On the way back we brushed our clothes and shaved our faces twice over. Then we carefully rehearsed the stories we were going to tell.

Passing the lighthouse, we flashed a message to Naval Intelligence announcing our return. Now, coming into the harbor, we could see—through our glasses—a considerable number of blue uniforms waiting for us at the dock. The skipper was convinced that he wouldn't lose anything but his command, Garbidge and Miller figured on just a few short years of detention, and I avoided thinking at all.

As soon as we docked, the port security officer came aboard and listened in silence while we told our stories. Then he stood up and said, "There may possibly be an element of truth in your stories, but in the entire history of the British Navy there is no precedent for a minesweeper serving as a hostel for immigrants."

With this he left, saying that the captain in charge of Belfast harbor would soon appear in person.

The captain showed up in no time, and said nothing while Garbidge, Miller, and the skipper reported. When my turn came, I started out by saying that it certainly wasn't the fault of Garbidge, Miller, or the skipper that I had been born in Hungary....

"Where was that?" he interrupted.

"Hungary," I repeated. "In Budapest."

The captain rubbed his hands. "My boy," he said, "you must have dinner with us tonight! Budapest! My wife was born there too!"

The skipper got a three-day shore leave. Garbidge and Miller were promised quick promotions. And I had a terrific Hungarian dinner, and was delivered—the next day—by special plane to London.

III

The press relations officer at the Admiralty in London received me with open pages of reports taken from a folder marked ROBERT CAPA. He looked at me, glanced at the reports, and said that he hoped my trip had been interesting. He also hoped I wouldn't make up funny stories the way newspapermen often do, but would stick to writing about the merchant marine. Rather casually, he threw in that the censor could not, of course, release any possible story of mine about minesweepers or Naval Intelligence, as it had not been part of my original assignment. Finally, just before I left, he told me that the *Collier's* office had been inquiring about my arrival and seemed rather anxious to see me.

The *Collier's* "office" turned out to be a big, luxurious suite in the Savoy Hotel occupied by Quentin Reynolds. He was having a cup of black coffee, and asked me to join him.

Cables and newspapers were strewn all over the room. The newspapers screamed about the invasion of North Africa, and the cables from the New York office yelled for Capa to proceed there at once. Reynolds nonchalantly asked me whether I had already been accredited to the Army, and I answered that not only had I not yet been accredited, but my chances of being accredited to the U.S. Army—indeed, to any army but the Hungarian—were practically nil. I pretended to be just as surprised as he that *Collier's* didn't know I was Hungarian. He asked me how soon I could go back to the States. I tried to convince him that I was potentially a great war photographer, and also pointed out that one way and another *Collier's* had spent about a thousand dollars getting me to London and might look unfavorably on my speedy return.

We agreed to continue the discussion over a couple of drinks. Downstairs, at the Savoy bar, after we had had only one drink, Quent gave in and admitted that it might be fun to have a Hungarian photographer around.

———

The first formality for every friendly or enemy alien in London during wartime was to register at the Vine Street police station. There was a long queue in front of the station when we arrived.

Now in 1942, except for Franklin D. Roosevelt, I suppose Quentin Reynolds was the most popular American in England. Quent had a big, soft heart raised in Brooklyn, and nourished in every bar where newspapermen hung out.

No one would have thought of letting his 220 pounds stand in a queue with ordinary, undersized aliens. Quent and I made a great theatrical entrance. He stopped at the threshold of the registration room, and—after an impressive pause—announced in the same voice in which he had made his famous broadcast to Dr. Goebbels and Schicklgruber, "I have brought you a German spy to register!" Then he turned to me and in his broken German said, *"Nicht wahr?"*

The audience reacted as he had expected. The whole police station was rolling with laughter. In no time, I was presented with a registration card, on which all the restrictions were promptly waived, and I became the King's and Quentin Reynolds' own enemy alien.

Opposite: LONDON, JUNE–JULY 1941. *Air-raid warden John Bramley takes his place as guard before Post 2 of the Lambeth district of London. Bramley was on twenty-four-hour duty during the Blitz.*

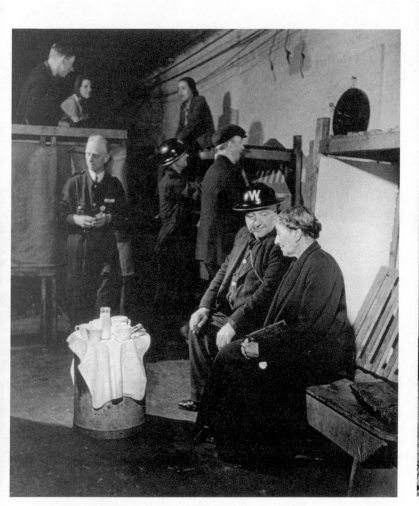

LONDON, JUNE–JULY 1941. *Teatime in an air-raid shelter.*

LONDON, JUNE–JULY 1941. *St. John's Church, in a heavily bombed Cockney neighborhood near Waterloo Road.*

LONDON, JUNE–JULY 1941. *Mrs. Gibbs, a resident of Whichcote Street, near Waterloo Road. Capa spent several days photographing the Gibbs family at home.*

LONDON, JUNE–JULY 1941. *A mum reads a letter from her enlisted son (note his photo, lower right).*

HERTFORDSHIRE, ENGLAND, 1942. *For her part in the war effort, a former London department store employee is in training to milk cows.*

Afterwards, the police inspector solicited us for Quent's autograph and a contribution to the Russian War Relief. The war was far from won, and England was still very grateful to the Russians.

Our next step was the Public Relations Office of the U.S. Army on Grosvenor Square. Our entrance was much quieter and our reception a bit colder. The major in charge of the P.R.O. did not think that my nationality did anything to simplify matters. If I received an assignment to do any pictures on the U.S. Army bases in England, he could give me a pass for facility visits, but I would have to be cleared by Intelligence before I could become regularly accredited to the American Army as a war correspondent. The word "Intelligence," otherwise known in mystery stories and military language as MIS, impressed the hell out of me. Quent took me over to a door with a big G-2 sign painted on it, wished me good luck, and advised me to be subdued, straightforward, and as little Hungarian as possible.

I expected to find some sort of inquisition, and was more than a little subdued. The "inquisition" I found was sitting behind a big desk. She was small and pert with a slightly upturned nose, and was surrounded by very pretty red hair. She was English, and was executive secretary to the chief.

I explained the object of my visit and wound up with a short history of my life. Indeed, I forgot all the good advice I had received, and behaved extremely Hungarian. She laughed at the end of my story, and remarked that I had very nice brown eyes and probably would look very well in an American uniform. We made a bargain: she would get me into the uniform and I would take her out in it the day I got it. She assured me she would fix everything, and I had a feeling that even my gray flannels would have been all right.

———

The next morning at the Savoy, a dignified waiter woke me up and brought me tea, cold powdered eggs, and three letters on a beautiful silver plate. He set down the tray on a table, where I had dumped the forty-eight rolls of still undeveloped film from my trip, my increasingly impressive bundle of identification papers, and some green dollar bills still left from the *Collier's* advance. Now I opened my letters leisurely. They reflected truly on my new situation of legality and prosperity. The American Army wrote that while waiting for accreditation I would be welcome to visit and photograph a group of Flying Fortresses based at the airfield at Chelveston. A weekly paper called *Illustrated* was greatly interested in acquiring the English rights to my stories, and offered me a hundred quid per story, sight unseen. And an English industrialist, a Mr. Yardley, whose wife, Flower, was the sister of a friend of mine in New York, sent me an invitation for the coming weekend or whenever I felt like it, to come out and stay with them at their place in Maidenhead.

Breakfast over, I dressed and decided to pay a visit to the London office of my former employers, *Time* and *Life*. *Life* had been my first big job, and a long time ago during the Spanish Civil War, when I first started working for them, I used to come up to London and the office had been very good to me.

The old gray building on Dean Street looked slightly disimproved as a result of the blitz. The pub next door, the Bath House, now had wooden panels instead of windows, but was still very much open for business. I began to feel all warm and sentimental.

Crocky and Dorothy, the two Irish girls who virtually ran the office five years ago, were still there. Crocky was now head researcher, but five years ago, when she was a secretary, she used to help me in Englishizing my English captions. She found that my English had improved to almost understandable since the last time I had been there. I showed her my article about the "Commodore of the Convoy," and my literary effort enthused her no end. She suggested doing a slight cleanup job on it, then spent the next four hours at the typewriter. In the meantime, for old times' sake, the darkroom of *Life* magazine developed the pictures I had taken for *Collier's*. Afterwards we all went down, and I tried to show my appreciation with pink gins at the Bath House.

———

Next morning, a messenger from *Life* delivered a hundred pictures and ten typewritten pages in triplicate of the "Commodore of the Convoy," all signed with my name. I sent one copy to the censor, one to *Collier's*, and took the third one over to the English picture magazine *Illustrated*. The editor of *Illustrated* looked at the pictures, read the story, and asked me if I had any objections to having my own face and biography printed with the story, and if the description "famous American photographer" would disturb me. Not very much, I answered. Then he gave me a check for 150 pounds.

I cashed the check at the Savoy and asked the doorman for the next train to Chelveston. Chelveston was a well-guarded English airfield occupied by the 301st Bomber Group of the young American air force. They had four dozen Flying Fortresses, some drab barracks, and an inheritance of knee-deep mud. My permit for a "facility visit" admitted me easily. The special services officer gave me an iron bed with three blankets, a Spam dinner, and left me in the middle of the mud outside the mess hall, telling me to make myself at home.

There I was in my civilian suit, and all around me were young uniforms who paid absolutely no attention to me. I didn't feel at home at all—indeed, I had no idea how to make myself at home there.

Everyone seemed to be heading toward one barracks in particular, and I decided to follow the trend. I entered the club room. I hoped desperately that somebody would talk to me. After a while, the Pfc behind the bar asked me what I wanted to drink. I felt very grateful and ordered warm beer like everyone else. The young flyers around me, among the first to fly the famous Fortresses over Europe, looked quiet and subdued. Some of them were reading old American magazines, others were sitting all alone writing endless letters. The only real activity seemed to be in the middle of the room, around a big table hidden by the backs of the guys crowded around it.

I edged in just in time to hear someone yell "High and low!" as he raked in a lot of money from the middle of the table. I watched the game for some time but couldn't figure out what they were playing. It must be some kind of poker, I finally decided, and definitely a game of skill! Soon one of the fellows got up and left the game. Here was my chance to make myself at home. I was graciously admitted. They dealt me two cards down and one card up and asked for half a crown. Then one at a time they dealt me three more cards up and finally another one down. After each card they asked for more money, and for the last card I had to pay two pounds. After all the cards had been dealt, the players started to declare themselves. Some of them said "high," some of them said "low." I studied my hand carefully— some of the cards had faces, some had low numbers. So I said, "High *and* low." I wasn't at all popular. They demanded that I show my three down cards. I did...they laughed...and two of them split the money in the pot.

After a while, I went back to my room to get my camera, and got even by taking pictures of the poker players. Also the magazine readers, the letter writers, the warm-beer drinkers, and the gramophone addicts.

At midnight the club room emptied—there was going to be a mission in the morning and the boys expected an early briefing. We were awakened at five and hurried over to the briefing room. One officer explained the weather conditions in detail; another went into the shape of the target; and a third talked at length about the amount of flak and the number of enemy fighters they could expect to encounter. At six, everyone was back in the club room, waiting for the signal to take off. The wait was long and nerve-racking. Nobody spoke a word. This was only the third mission over Europe.

At nine, the loudspeaker announced that the ceiling over France had closed in...that everybody could go back to bed. The boys were angry and disappointed. They returned to the mud, the magazines, the letters, the warm beer, and the poker.

This same routine went on for four days. I took a lot of pictures. I practiced up on my high-low and also learned some fascinating new poker games called "spit-in-the-ocean," "baseball," and "red dog." By the fifth morning, I was completely out of pounds, but this time the mission wasn't scrubbed. I accompanied my poker chums to their planes and took pictures of them from every angle. A young lieutenant named Bishop was the last to take off, and before climbing to

Opposite: CHELVESTON, ENGLAND, NOVEMBER 1942. *An American 301st Bomber Group formation leader and his crew listen intently during a briefing prior to a daylight raid on St. Nazaire, from which U-boats were being sent to menace American shipping to North Africa.*

CHELVESTON, ENGLAND, NOVEMBER 1942. *A navigator of the American 301st Bomber Group.*

the controls he posed for a portrait. He was just a little guy, but his nose bore an amazing resemblance to the nose of his ship, so I posed them together. I was very pleased with the composition.

The planes took off. I waited for six long hours in the control tower before the first returning Fortress appeared on the horizon. As they approached we started to count them. In the morning there had been twenty-four ships in beautiful formation. Now, counting all over the sky, there were only seventeen.

They circled over the control tower and waited for permission to land. One of the ships had had its landing gear shot away, and had wounded aboard. The tower ordered it to come in first and attempt a belly landing. I got my Contax ready and got one roll of film used up by the time the plane came to a safe standstill. I ran up to the plane and focused my second Contax. The hatch opened, and what was left of a guy was handed down to the waiting medics. He was still moaning. The next two didn't moan anymore. The last man to leave the plane was the pilot. He seemed to be all right except for a slight gash on his forehead. I moved to get a close-up. He stopped midway and cried, "Are these the pictures you were waiting for, photographer?" I shut my camera and left for London without saying good-bye.

On the train to London, with those successfully exposed rolls in my bag, I hated myself and my profession. This sort of photography was only for undertakers, and I didn't like being one. If I was to share the funeral, I swore, I would have to share the procession.

—

Next morning, after sleeping it over, I felt better. While shaving, I held a conversation with myself about the incompatibility of being a reporter and hanging on to a tender soul at the same time. The pictures of the guys sitting around the airfield without the pictures of their being hurt and killed would have given the wrong impression. The pictures of the dead and wounded were the ones that would show people the real aspect of war, and I was glad I had taken that one roll before I turned soppy.

Illustrated called to find out about my story, and I volunteered that it was "sensational." They said they would send someone over immediately to pick up the negatives and develop them in their darkroom.

I hadn't forgotten the airfield and was more anxious than ever to get into uniform. I took Pat, the redheaded secretary of the U.S. Army Intelligence, out to lunch, to see if my accreditation couldn't be speeded up. She told me that my accreditation was being favorably considered and that I wouldn't be risking much in ordering a United States war correspondent's uniform from my tailor.

The tailor had definite ideas as to how an American officer's uniform ought to look. The material was somewhat different in color from regulation—but much prettier, I thought. I hoped my accreditation would come through in six days—and the tailor said my uniform would be ready by that time.

I went back to the *Collier's* office to report the good news to Quentin Reynolds. He added some of his own: *Collier's* had received my convoy story in New York and would run it in a four-page spread. I told him about my visit to the air force, and he cautioned me against trying to do too much too fast. He suggested instead that I go out and get acquainted with the spirit of London, following this up with several addresses and a few hints as to where the spirit might be found.

The spirit of London, just after the blitz but before the full American invasion of England, was open and inviting. I found it in no time at all...and something else too. Somehow the spirit persisted and the something else continued for six days and through the strangest places—none of which included the Savoy. God created the world in six days, and on the seventh, the hangover....

I was looking forward to bed when I opened the door to my room at the Savoy. I had visitors. Pacing up and down in my room were Mr. Spooner, the editor of *Illustrated,* and an American Army major. The major clutched a copy of *Illustrated* in his hand. He stuck the paper under my nose and stabbed at the cover with his finger.

"Did you take this picture? Do you realize what you've done?"

I recognized the picture on the cover immediately. It was my favorite of all the shots I had taken out at the airfield. It had come out very well.

"Sure," I answered. "That's Lieutenant Bishop and his Fortress."

"The hell with Lieutenant Bishop!" he yelled. His angry finger

pointed to a little black thing in the nose of the Fortress. The little black thing looked like nothing to me, but by then I knew that it had all the earmarks of disaster. The major didn't keep me very long in suspense.

"That little black thing! That's the A-number-one secret of the American air force!" He almost choked. "That's the Norden bomb-sight!"

I hadn't known. The air crews always had strict orders to keep that little black thing covered when not in actual operation. Bishop's bombardier had lifted the canvas five minutes too soon. I tried to explain that my only interest in the nose of the Fortress had been its resemblance to Lieutenant Bishop's nose. Spooner explained that inasmuch as he had been unable to reach me during the past week so that I could clear the story with American censorship, he had shown the pictures to the RAF censors. They had had nothing against that little black thing.

This revealing issue of *Illustrated* was due to appear on the news-stands in another three days. Spooner offered to recall and destroy the 400,000 copies that were already printed and awaiting distribution.

"That may save you, Mr. Spooner," the major said, "but it doesn't save Capa. He had no right to even show you his pictures until he had first passed them through American censorship."

Spooner hurried away to stop his presses and halt distribution. The major put me under house arrest and left to make his report to headquarters. I collapsed on my bed, next to a box containing my new war correspondent's uniform. I was sure I would never have to open that box. But I was wrong. That afternoon, the American Public Relations Office notified me that they had been obliged to accredit me—inasmuch as unaccredited civilians are not subject to court-martial.

I opened the box.

———

The following morning I appeared for a preliminary hearing before a board consisting of public relations and intelligence officers. It was their job to determine what I would be charged with in court-martial.

When I arrived, the first thing I realized was that any resemblance between my uniform and theirs was purely coincidental. I was afraid that this was the straw that would finish the camel.

I proclaimed my innocence in great detail and with considerable heat, but the hotter I got, the less English it sounded. They stopped me cold in the middle of my innocence and began to argue among themselves. I could understand *them* very clearly. They were on the verge of some sort of agreement when the door opened and the chief PRO walked in, followed by my Lieutenant Bishop.

Bishop took the floor and slyly assured them that I didn't—couldn't—tell an ace from a deuce, nor a Norden bombsight from a tin of C-rations, and that the whole case obviously had been engineered by a gremlin. My desk-jobbed jury couldn't argue against flying Bishops at this early fighting stage. I was reprimanded, dismissed—and accredited. Bishop and I proceeded to a pub.

"By the way," he asked me, "what is the address of your tailor?"

———

The whole *Collier's* office and the bar at the Savoy Hotel were very impressed with my uniform. It was sort of an American cut, they finally agreed, and sort of a British Colonial color. I decided to celebrate.

I invited Pat, the red-haired secretary, to the promised dinner and we drank champagne. After the second bottle, Pat couldn't remember who I was anymore, and after the third, she forgot her own name and address. I knew that if I didn't get her home, this time it would take a priest—not a Bishop—to wind up the affair.

We got into a taxi and Pat passed out. I tried to wake her up, but she was out cold. I had only a pound note left and watched the taxi meter with growing anxiety. I shook Pat again. When I looked up, the taxi meter read one pound, ten. I searched my pockets. Then I searched Pat. In her purse I found two pounds and also a membership card to a bottle party giving her name and address. I stopped the taxi by the Serpentine in Hyde Park, dipped Pat's head twice in the water, and delivered her home.

I was very drunk, very happy, very virtuous, proud of myself, and very much resolved not to drink, gamble, or have anything to do with redheaded girls anymore.

LONDON, JANUARY–FEBRUARY 1943. *An American officer entertains the war orphans "adopted" by his unit.*

I wanted to be very sure. I stumbled to my desk and wrote a note to War Correspondent Capa: "No drinks. No gambling. No bombsights. No girls." I placed the paper on my uniform blouse and blissfully passed out.

Next morning, my head was splitting. I couldn't remember what had happened until I found the piece of paper, decided that the best way to keep out of trouble was to avoid it, and made up my mind to visit with the Yardleys in the country until my departure for North Africa. I left my phone number with the desk, and took the train to Maidenhead.

Once I arrived at the Yardleys' place I knew I would be safe. I'd be reading mystery stories by the fireplace, arguing about the war and Russia with Mr. Yardley, and going to sleep at nine in the evening.

—

They were very happy to see me in such a pretty uniform and hinted that maybe some food and black coffee could make further improvements. We sat down at the table: the Yardleys, their house guest, and I. The guest—a young girl—sat next to me, but I was not looking at women, certainly not when they were pale blondes and kind of fat. After coffee, I explained that I was in unusual shape that day, due to the celebrations in honor of my uniform, and that all I needed to be happy was a big chair and a good book.

I got into the big chair, opened the good book, and fell asleep. Ten minutes later I was awakened by the loud grinding of the gramophone. The little round house guest was playing Tino Rossi. I told her wryly I hated Tino Rossi, and noticed that she was really not very fat. She was wearing slacks and a sweater, and I thought she might have a rather good figure. Also, her hair was not really blonde, but kind of goldish pink. I promptly closed my eyes. She turned Tino Rossi a little louder, and when I opened my eyes she was standing against the light. Her profile was rather delicately English, and it seemed she had gray-green slit eyes. I got up and went out on the terrace to sleep.

When I got up again, a big fire was going in the living-room fireplace, and the gramophone was playing a rumba. The house guest was now wearing a tight-fitting black dress.

"My name is Elaine," she told me. I had an idea I would have a hard time closing my eyes this time, and was very glad that I was a bad dancer and could hold on to my good resolutions. She said she hoped I preferred the rumba to Tino Rossi, and I told her the facts about my dancing. To prove my honesty, I offered to dance with her once. She said my rumba wasn't really bad and could be improved in no time. I answered that in ten years no one had succeeded in making any improvements. She said she had a brand-new idea. I was afraid I had one too.

The Yardleys had come down and inquired how I liked my book. I was forced to admit that I was wasting my time learning to dance the rumba. Especially, I added, since nobody danced the rumba in North Africa, and I was practically on my way there.

The pink-haired girl remarked that it would be a great pity if I were to die without ever having learned how to dance, and the Yardleys agreed.

We had a bottle of champagne to North Africa, my rumba definitely improved, and I began to call the girl Pinky. She didn't seem to mind very much, but stopped the gramophone, picked up my book, and started to read. I went back to the gramophone and started Tino Rossi.

The Yardleys started to laugh and figured they had better go to bed. Pinky looked up from her book at me and said, "I think you are an utter fool."

I answered, "I think you are an utter teaser." She told me that that was not good English, after which I told her that her lips tasted of strawberries.

"There aren't many strawberries in England," she said, "but the few grown here are famed to be excellent. And anyway, I'm not teasing."

I knew then that she was not teasing. I was happy she existed, and that I had found her.

The telephone rang, and it rang for me. It was the Savoy, saying they had been trying to get me for the past two hours, that a Captain Chris Scott from the American P.R.O. had been calling every five minutes. I put down the receiver and asked Pinky to drive me to the station.

In the car I told her how happy I was about going to North Africa; that I was a gypsy and a newspaperman, besides being an enemy alien; that I was very sorry and very glad—because she was far too lovely. She said absolutely nothing, just let me out of the car at the station, and drove quickly away without saying good-bye.

Chris Scott, who was a very nice young captain, said he was sorry I had rushed up in the middle of the night, as tomorrow would have been time enough. I told him that in some ways I was glad, and that his call had reached me just in time, because all I wanted to do was go to North Africa. I told him about Pinky.

He brought out a bottle of Scotch and proposed a drink to my lucky escape. I told him it really tasted better than strawberries. Pointedly, he remarked that he liked strawberries, and that while I was going to North Africa, he was probably staying in London. All I knew, I told him, was that she ought to be called Pinky, and that I had forgotten to ask her full name or her telephone number.

Chris said that was too bad—and I discovered not only that I was sorry I didn't know her name, address, or telephone number, but also that if I had them I wouldn't have given them away.

The following morning I called the Yardleys to say thanks and good-bye. Nonchalantly, I asked if Elaine was near the telephone, but Mr. Yardley said she had already left for town. He didn't volunteer any further information, and I didn't ask for any.

My day was very busy. The American Army gave me orders: the British gave me an exit permit. They told me I would need a new visa if I ever wanted to get back, and that, unfortunately, even in an American uniform I was technically a Hungarian citizen.

My train to Glasgow, where I was to board ship, was leaving from Euston Station at 7:30 that evening. I arrived far too early, decided I had a right to celebrate my departure, and looked for the bar. It was very crowded. The only empty place was at a table where a girl was sitting all alone. She was not fat; she was not blonde; she had pink hair. She looked up at me and said, "I hoped you would be early." She didn't tell me how she had found out about my train. I asked the barmaid if she had any champagne. She had a very good bottle. We toasted, and Pinky started to sing a corny French song, "*J'attendrai.*"

The barmaid was getting very sentimental, and by the time we got to my train it was time to go aboard. A naval bloke was taking up the whole window to kiss his girl good-bye. The train was ready to move, so I yelled at the guy, "Let's split it!"

Without turning his head, he replied, "Yank, I'm not splitting my girl with anyone."

I said, "Not the girl—the window!"

He moved over and I barely made it. It still tasted like strawberries. I sat back in my compartment, and didn't know her name and telephone number.

IV

SPRING 1943

I arrived in Algiers aboard a regular troopship carrying a fresh Scottish division to North Africa as reinforcements for the spring campaign and the long overdue taking of Tunis.

By the time our boat docked, I was very much used to my uniform. So was everyone else. Everyone on board expected strange and mysterious things of war, and I—and my accent—became one of those strange and mysterious things.

This time, nobody wanted to take away my cameras, question my existence, or ask for any passports. The public relations officer in Algiers told me that the war was hundreds of miles away in the hills of Tunisia—with a big offensive due to start at any minute. I was provided with a jeep, a bedding roll, and a driver, and we started out. I hoped I would be able to catch up with the war.

We drove night and day, and finally arrived at Army headquarters in Feriana. But the big attack had already got under way, and our armor had broken through at Gafsa.

Depressed by the unexpected quickness of war, I started out with my driver to chase after the 1st Armored Division. After driving all day, we arrived in the village of Gafsa. I had finally caught up with at least the tail end of the war. I decided to get a good night's sleep before starting out on my pursuit after the forward elements.

The Army billeted me in an Arab schoolhouse. The floor of the dark schoolroom was covered with bedrolls, and only one spot—the one closest to the wall—was unoccupied. I undid my bedroll and crawled in. I had a dream. I caught up with the armored division just before the gates of Tunis and jumped on the leading tank.... I was the only photographer to get a picture of Rommel's capture ... in the center of town, a shell exploded ... my face was scorched....

I woke up and tried to open my eyes. My face burned violently and my eyes wouldn't open. Sometime during my heroic dream I must have got hurt. I yelled for help, and heard someone walk up to my bedroll.

"What did you expect, you stupid so-and-so?" he asked. "Don't you know that in an Arab house, right next to the wall, you're the bedbug's best bet?"

I pushed my swollen eyelids open with my fingers, hid my face behind dark glasses, and went out to search for my driver.

We got back on the road. I began to dislike this war. The life of a war correspondent wasn't so romantic. We drove for hours over a slow, bumpy road through the empty desert. We met no living soul, of either friendly or enemy extraction. All we found were a few pieces of useless equipment left behind by the Germans.

It became by now a pressing matter to stop my jeep. But after the previous night's experience, I didn't feel inclined to visit the toilet of an Arab cultural institution. There were definitely no girls around, and with my blurry eyes I didn't want to go too far from the jeep. I made out an inviting clump of cactus a few yards from the road and ran toward it.

There was nothing wrong with my African cactus except for a little wooden signpost which grew in its shadow. It grew very fast and opened my eyes wide. The sign was in German, but very easy to understand. Through my black glasses, I read: "ACHTUNG! MINEN!"

Opposite: EL GUETTAR, TUNISIA, MARCH 1943.

MAKNASSY, TUNISIA, MARCH 22, 1943. *An American soldier shares a cigarette with a local resident.*

I did not jump, I did not stir. I did not dare to do anything. I had to do something very badly, but it takes very little to make a land mine go off. I shouted my predicament to my driver. I told him I was standing in the middle of a minefield. He seemed to think the situation was funny. I could see no cause for laughter. I didn't dare to retrace my footsteps, because the mines that had failed to go off the first time might have changed their minds by now. I urged him to drive off and bring back somebody with a mine detector.

I was caught with my pants down. There I was, braving death in a lonely, empty, soundless desert, standing nailed to the sand, behind a stupid cactus bush. Even my obituary would be unprintable.

Hours later, my driver returned with a mine removal squad and a *Life* photographer. The *Life* man took pictures while I was being de-mined. He told me that our attack had been halted, and that this would undoubtedly prove to be the most interesting picture of the day.

Rommel's crack armored division, the Hermann Goering, had been brought up to stop our advance. The disappointed newspapermen had returned and had set up camp in a small oasis a few miles outside of Gafsa.

In the evening, back at the press camp, my story was already famous. The correspondents were not yet allowed to write about the stopped war, and my little adventure became the favorite subject in the "letters home" department. Seeing them all writing to their wives and sweethearts, I thought of Pinky. I was relieved, though, that I didn't know her address. I didn't think my adventure had been exactly dashing.

———

Around midnight, the generators that supplied light in the tents of the oasis press camp began to cough, and we turned in. I made sure there were no mines or bedbugs in my corner of the Sahara, and I didn't intend to have any dreams. I had a dream. There were red and green flares hanging in the dark sky...red bullets...bursting bombs...all sorts of fantastic things. I turned over in my sleeping bag.

Next morning, when I woke up, there wasn't any tent over me.

The camp had been bombed during the night. The blasts had blown away all the tents, although no one was hurt. I was the object of envy and admiration for having slept through it all without stirring. The minefield episode was forgiven and forgotten.

———

Time magazine's Bill Lang and the GI's Ernie Pyle, both old-timers of the North African campaign, took me with them in their jeep. They promised to find me as much war as I needed for my health and my pictures. This time the road was better and much shorter. We headed for El Guettar, where the 1st Infantry Division was holding back the main German counterattack.

We found plenty of war before we reached the front. German fighter planes were strafing the road and every few minutes we had to stop the jeep and jump into a ditch for cover.

There was a lot of excitement, but I got no pictures at all.

Bill and Ernie stopped at division headquarters. I was in a hurry to get my first pictures and they told me to go on ahead and cross two little jebels (what the Arabs call their hills) and hide between the jebels in the wadi (the Arab word for valley). "Just ask anybody where the war is," they said. "You can't miss it."

I found jebels and wadies. The 16th Infantry Regiment was dug in and the GI's were writing letters and reading pocket books in deep foxholes. I asked them where the war was. They pointed to the next jebel. In every wadi, they pointed up to a jebel, and on every jebel, they pointed down a wadi.

Finally, on the last and highest hilltop, I found about fifty soldiers relaxing and heating up cans of C-rations. Their faces were devoid of all enthusiasm. I walked up to their lieutenant and asked where all the shooting was. "It's hard to say," he answered. "My platoon has only the most advanced position on the front."

He consoled me with a can of C-rations. Just as I was about to dig

Opposite: EL GUETTAR, TUNISIA, MARCH 23, 1943. *On this day American troops, under General George S. Patton, engaged in a dramatic tank and infantry battle that resulted in the war's first decisive American victory over the Germans.*

into the awful-looking stew, a shell whistled and I threw myself flat on the ground, spilling the meat and beans all over me. It was a German shell all right, but it landed a few hundred yards away. When I raised my head, the lieutenant—who hadn't budged—was looking down at me. He was very smug. Sheepishly I got up, dusted off the beans, and told him that from my angle this war was like an aging actress: more and more dangerous, and less and less photogenic.

With the next whistle, the lieutenant ducked too. The Germans were giving us the real McCoy. First they shaved the top of our hill with their artillery, then they advanced with fifty tanks and two infantry regiments right to the foot of our jebel. Now our tank destroyers moved out and began to slug it out right in open sight.

Three generals joined us in our grandstand seat to cheer the team. Patton, who commanded II Corps, and Terry Allen and Teddy Roosevelt, who were in command of the 1st Division. After every hit on a German tank, Patton bubbled with delight under his three-star helmet; Terry Allen picked up a walkie-talkie and coached his team personally; and Teddy Roosevelt swung his cane happily.

Late in the afternoon, the Germans withdrew, leaving behind twenty-four burned-out tanks and a lot of very dead krauts.

I got all kinds of pictures; pictures of dust, pictures of smoke, and of generals; but none of the tension and drama of battle, which I could feel and follow with my naked eyes.

———

Our breakthrough to the sea and Tunis was bogged down, but we managed to stop the Germans from pushing us back and retaking Gafsa. The 1st Division fought for three weeks on the jebels of El Guettar, and every day I took the same pictures of dust, smoke, and death.

After sundown, we would return to the press camp. The correspondents typed their stories and I shipped my pictures. No one discussed the events of the day. We drank Algerian wine and talked about "that woman at home." Each of us told about his own girl—always the most exciting and marvelous one in the world. Then they always dragged out a blurred, undistinguishable snapshot to prove it.

I told them simply that my girl was pink.

That worn-out bunch of unromantic scribes, who had been listening with straight faces to the lies glorifying and beautifying that blurred girl at home, burst out into disgusting laughter. They said that pink women didn't exist, and that I ought to have the decency to lie honorably about blondes, brunettes, and redheads like everyone else. I had no snapshot to prove my claim.

But a few mornings later, the courier who brought our mail from Algiers had a package for me. There, wrapped in tissue paper, was an English doll, a doll with pink hair. The existence of my pink girl was never questioned again.

—

Scaling the same jebels and taking the same pictures around El Guettar day after day was a fruitless and dangerous routine. So when I received an offer to fly in a plane instead of walk up mountains, and to continue my education in the manly art of poker, I gladly accepted. The offer came from my old friend Lieutenant Bishop, who wrote me that his group—the 301st Bombardiers—had been transferred to North Africa, and was allowed to take war correspondents for a ride in every respect.

The Fortresses were battered; the pilots had a lot of ribbons; only the poker game was the same. I was the same too, and lost heavily the first night.

In the morning, we went on a mission to bomb the German shipping concentrated in the harbor of Bizerte. I flew with Lieutenant Jay, who had been the big winner in the poker game the night before. I figured he would want to protect his winnings carefully.

Our Fortress was called *The Goon.* Bishop's *Gremlin* flew on our right, our wings almost touching. It was nice and dull in the air. The oxygen bottles cured our hangovers and the cold air at 20,000 feet was welcome change from the heat below.

Over the target, things became less dull and much warmer. The explosions of the ack-ack guns rocked our plane; the black puffs of the shells formed a carpet right below us and we rocked on it. We kept a straight formation until we were right above the ships and released our eggs from our open belly. Then Bishop yelled through the intercom "high and low" and we broke formation. We swerved and dived and then climbed again, leaving the little black puffs and the big smoke of the burning ships behind us. We flew low over the sea, took off the oxygen bottles, and gave up the bored act. We joked and were visibly relieved.

All the poker players returned and we played again. I didn't get back my money and decided to stay for one more day. For five days I flew. Over Tunis, Naples, Bizerte, and my luck didn't change at all. Then we got a new target: Palermo. The ack-ack was much worse here than it had been before, and two squadrons of German fighters were up in the air waiting for us. They were like little silver dots above us in the sky, then they shook their shiny wings and dived and grew into ugly spitting monsters. Their bullets tore holes in our wings with the precision of a sewing machine, and *The Goon* was nearly down. Lieutenant Jay straightened the plane almost on the sea. Three of our motors were still going strong and we made home without much trouble.

Most of the planes were in ahead of us. We waited for the others on the landing strip until late after darkness, and that night we did not play. One of our partners was missing.

Next day I left the group and, having accomplished five missions over enemy territory, was recommended for the Air Medal. I almost deserved the Purple Heart—for the five nights at poker.

———

During the time I flew with the Fortresses I managed to miss our final successful attack. The Germans suddenly crumbled and our armies entered Tunis.

Victory was pleasant and exhausting. During the day in the streets of Tunis we were kissed by hundreds of old women and drank many glasses of wine. We found a nice apartment in a big, modern building where we finished our stories and really started to celebrate. We had enough liquor from a captured Gestapo warehouse to keep our singing throats from drying out.

About midnight there was a rap on the door and a dignified French citizen entered the room. "Messieurs!" he cried. "For three months you have been bombing us every night. That was all right,

TUNISIA, APRIL 1943. *American fighter ace, with nine German shootdowns and one Italian to his credit.*

CONSTANTINE, ALGERIA, MAY 1943. *Men of the U.S. 301st Bomber Group after a daylight mission. The plane's landing gear had been shot away, but the pilot managed to make a successful belly landing.*

c'est la guerre. But peace has been declared now, and my wife and little daughter wish to sleep."

We poured a glass of German brandy down the bravely resisting Frenchman's throat, and promised that peace would definitely be declared tomorrow. I fished the pink doll out of my bag and presented it to the Frenchman for his sleepy little daughter.

The hangovers of victory are strong and painful. Our war was finished for the moment. We had absolutely no liquor left, and all the pretty girls in Tunis were kept locked in their rooms by their fathers.

We were heating our K-ration coffee and preparing some breakfast, when Bill Lang took me aside. He said he had information that it would be at least four weeks before the next invasion, that the war would be a long one, and that it was dangerous to leave girls pining away in London. He added that there was a boat leaving for England in five days.

Two days later I sat in the waiting room at the British Consulate in Algiers. The consul was a typical, dried-out civil servant. He was obviously very bored with both the French and the Arabs, and didn't want to be bothered with Yanks either.

"You are an American. You're in the Army. You have travel orders. You don't need a visa."

"I am not an American. I am only very close to the Army, and I need a visa badly."

He looked over the document which the British consul had put together for me in New York. "Highly irregular," he remarked drily. "The liberties taken by some of our consulates are difficult to understand." He didn't look up. "What are your reasons for wanting to go to England?"

"Purely sentimental, sir."

"I grant you four weeks. The fee is one pound, ten shillings."

V

Sixteen days later, after many delays, Bill Lang and I docked in Liverpool on a Sunday morning. It was early afternoon by the time we got to London, and there we parted. Bill took off to the very best hotel, and I took the train to Maidenhead.

It was a Sunday once more, and the Yardleys' place looked just as it did six months before. But this time, when I knocked on the door, I was a bit more anxious. Mr. Yardley opened it. "You're just in time for tea!"

The fire was lit in the living room. They had a house guest, but she was not pink. They asked me how it was in North Africa. I told them that the war there was boring. They answered politely that the war in England was very boring too. I edged slowly toward the gramophone. Mrs. Yardley watched me without turning her head. Casually, she asked me, "Did your rumba technique improve while you were in North Africa?"

"I may need a few more lessons," I answered lightly.

"I have an idea you'll get them."

The subject was dropped, but I felt much better. We talked about the weather and the food rations. During a pause in the conversation, I picked up a Tino Rossi record. I turned to Yardley. "By the way," I asked, "what happened to that blondish girl who used to like these awful records?"

"Elaine Parker? As a matter of fact, she hasn't been playing them lately. She would be here today, but this is the Sunday when she has night duty over at the Ministry of Information. That's where she works, you know."

After dinner, I said that I had to return to London. Nobody tried to detain me. The trip from Maidenhead to London was longer than North Africa to England.

I called the Ministry of Information from the station and was informed that Miss Parker was in the American Division and would come on duty at midnight. Two more hours....

I found Bill at Claridge's, where he had got two bedrooms and a living room for us. His girl's telephone hadn't answered all day. He presumed I hadn't been any luckier and offered to share his decanter of whisky. Then he looked at me again.

"I have a date at midnight," I said.

And then I started to clean myself of six months of North African dirt. At midnight I picked up the telephone, asked for the proper extension, and listened.

"American Division—Miss Parker speaking."

"What color is your hair, Miss Parker?"

"Who is speaking?"

"What's your favorite song, Miss Parker?"

"Where are you?"

"I think I'm slightly in love."

"Does it hurt?"

"I'll meet you over at your canteen in fifteen minutes."

When she came into the canteen, I was standing at the bar, resting my head on my elbows, staring at the bottles in front of me. She walked directly to the bar, put her elbows on it, and said:

"Hello."

"Your hair is still pink."

"If you'd made me wait much longer, you'd have found it all gray."

"Were you waiting?"

"No, I got married and had six children."

"I hope they will like me."

We turned around and walked out of the bar without touching our drinks. We walked around the building, and when she broke away, she said:

"Be at the entrance at eight in the morning." Then she ran away.

The streets of London are gray and empty at eight in the morning. We found a teashop and she ordered bacon, tomatoes, tea, and toast. By now both of us were very serious.

"Did you come back because I was waiting for you?"

"Yes."

"Are you going to stay?"

"No."

"Do you like bacon and tomatoes?"

"I'd like to stay."

I told her I had to return to war, but then I'd be back. I explained that besides what might happen in war, my own situation was so uncertain that I never knew what might happen the following day.

"I am very pretty."

"Who told you so?"

"People who drop in."

"Why were you waiting for me?"

"I made up my mind the first minute I saw you."

"Still not teasing?"

"Please pay the bill."

It was 9:00 A.M. and I had to go over to the *Collier's* office to check in and tell them I was taking a seven-day vacation. Pinky thought she could arrange to take her vacation at the same time. We started for the Savoy together.

Collier's was still at the Savoy, but Quent was no longer there and the man who replaced him said he had a cable for me from the New York office. It was addressed to me and read:

YOUR NORTH AFRICAN PICTURES WONDERFUL STOP WAR DEPARTMENT
INSISTING ON POOL REGULATIONS STOP THEREFORE AVAILABLE TO ALL
PAPERS STOP YOUR PICTURES USED BY EVERYONE BEFORE WE COULD
PRINT THEM STOP REGRET HAVE TO RECALL YOU TO NEW YORK STOP
WILL PAY TRAVELING EXPENSES PLUS THREE WEEKS ADDITIONAL
SALARY

COLLIERS NEW YORK

I read it over three times, and then gave it to Pinky. I asked the *Collier's* man when he had received it. That same morning, he told me. I asked him whether anyone else knew about it yet. He said no, and I had to think fast. If I lost my job I would also lose my accreditation as a war correspondent. I would have to go back to the States, and with my papers what they were, I would never get out again. I just had to get a new job before the Army found out I'd been fired. I explained my situation to the *Collier's* man. He said he was sorry but he didn't think there was anything he could do about it. I asked him to wait until noon to give me time to go around to some of the other magazines and see what my chances were. He was reluctant, but he didn't say no.

"You go ahead," said Pinky. "I'll wait for you here."

I took a taxi to *Life* magazine.

My relations with *Life* were far from excellent. During the six years I had worked for them, they had fired me twice and I had quit once. But my relations with Crocky, who was in charge of the London office, were of long standing and more than good. She was pleased to see me again, and was not too surprised to hear that I was in trouble. She said that my chances of getting a job straight away were very poor, and she thought that the New York office, hearing that I was out of a job again, would just think that I ought to be used to it by now. However, she had information that big things would be brewing pretty soon along the Mediterranean, and thought that if I could get back to North Africa before the Army learned I had been fired, and if I could somehow pull a fast one and scoop the rest of the photographers, then the thing might be wangled somehow. It all seemed perfectly simple—just this side of impossible—but I had to give it a try.

Crocky cabled *Life* in New York that she had heard that Capa was extremely dissatisfied with *Collier's* and could be persuaded to quit.

I took a taxi back to the Savoy. When I entered the *Collier's* office, Pinky was sitting on the bureau right beside the telephone. Over in a corner of the room was the poor *Collier's* representative, close to a nervous breakdown.

I said it was all fixed, and if he didn't tell the Army I'd been fired for forty-eight hours, he could be godfather to my children. If we would just get out of his office, he answered, it would be at least seventy-two hours before he could think or mention our names again.

Close to the Savoy is the best restaurant in London, the Boulestin. I had to talk to Pinky, so we went there for lunch. Boulestin still had very good French champagne, and I proposed a toast to my getting away.

"How soon?"

"Tonight. It has to be."

Her eyes filled up with champagne. I told her about my scheme with *Life* and that I thought I might be able to swing the air reservation through my friend Chris Scott over at the air force P.R.O. As soon as lunch was over, I called the P.R.O. Chris Scott had been transferred somewhere in North Africa!

Pinky put her little finger in her mouth and chewed on it twice.

"I think I know how to fix it."

She told me to go ahead and get my exit permit and meet her at 5:30 at the Mayfair Club.

The security officer at the Passport Office was highly suspicious about my arriving in England on Sunday and wanting to leave on Monday. I told him I couldn't give him any details which concerned military operations. He was quite impressed, and I had no more trouble.

Pinky arrived at the Mayfair Club at six o'clock, ordered a drink and said:

"You can go now. I have your reservation."

I had to be at the air terminal at 6:30. I told her I would come back to England soon.

"Well, you'd better."

I asked her what she was going to do tonight after I left.

"You black-hearted Hungarian dope! I'm having dinner with the officer who gave you that air priority—to make my evening free!"

She kissed me lightly, and ran away.

In the dark airplane, flying from England to North Africa, I was very sure that I was very much in love with Pinky. And this time I knew her name and address. I even had her picture.

VI

The white city of Algiers looked even whiter from the air, and the blue harbor was black, jammed with boats of all kinds and sizes.

At Eisenhower's public relations headquarters, the pressroom was deserted, the usual crowd of newspapermen vanished, and the press officers gone. I tried to find out what was cooking but the few sergeants on duty were noncommittal. They would say only that the P.R.O. officers were at Eisenhower's campaign headquarters. I asked them to connect me on a direct wire. It couldn't be done, they said; headquarters had been sealed since the day before.

I put a few numbers together and figured out that the invasion of somewhere was going to happen any minute, much faster than I had expected. I was too late. I was left out of the invasion, and I would get no scoop and no new job. The news of my being fired would catch up with me right in Algiers. After all the ado, I had gained nothing. Instead of from London, I would be shipped home from here.

I hung around the P.R.O., hoping desperately for my usual miracle. It happened in the men's room. I found there a war photographer, a colleague of mine, in very sad shape. He had the "GI's," or C-ration diarrhea, and was so much on the run that he had to stay in one place. He told me he had been trained for several months for a very special job: to jump with an airborne division on their first big mission. He had been assigned to the invasion, but had got so sick that they had sent him back at the last moment.

He was rather philosophical about the whole thing. He didn't particularly like parachute jumping anyway. Here was my chance to save two birds with one case of "GI's," and I asked how I might be able to replace him. He sent a message to airborne headquarters, they sent a plane to get me, and I was flown to a big improvised airfield near Kairouan in the middle of the Tunisian desert, where hundreds of transport planes and gliders were lined up and ready for the takeoff.

I was shown to the public relations tent, and there was my London friend, Captain Chris Scott, who was now the public relations officer for the 9th Troop Carrier Command. I told him my whole story.

"So you are still an enemy alien, Capa? Still chasing pink girls?" I showed him the picture of Pinky. He looked at it for some time. "It's really too bad that you're going to be killed in this invasion. I'll have to fly back to London and break the sad news to the pink girl. But for you, Capa, I'll do it."

He took me over to Major General Ridgway, the commander of the 82d Airborne Division, and introduced me. The general was very friendly.

"As long as you're willing to jump and take pictures of my division in combat, I don't care whether you're Hungarian, Chinese, or anything else. Have you ever jumped before?"

"No, sir."

"Well, it isn't natural, but there's nothing to it."

Back in his tent, Chris gave me the whole dope. The destination was Sicily. The 82d Airborne Division would be flown in by the 9th TCC six hours before the main seaborne landing. We were scheduled to jump at 1:00 A.M., and the barges would hit the beach by daybreak.

Chris had an idea. I would fly in the lead plane and take flash pictures of the paratroopers both during the flight and as they jumped. I wouldn't jump myself but would return to Kairouan with the empty transport plane. If I took the picture of the first man to jump,

I would have the picture of the first American to land in Sicily. My plane would get back to the base by 3:00 A.M. We would develop and radio the pictures to America and they would be there before the news of the invasion itself. My pictures would hit the presses simultaneously with the first big headlines.

The plan appealed to me in every detail. I began to like Chris very much.

In a short while we were called in for the official briefing. The planning staff outlined to the pilots and paratroop officers the different phases of the operation. They told us that when we reached the target we could expect a lot of flak and a lot of Germans. This is where we would "discover our souls." They made sure that everyone understood what he was supposed to do and we were trucked over to the waiting planes.

Chris said good-bye and told me he would wait for my return on the airfield. I didn't give him Pinky's picture, but—just in case—I gave him her address. We took off.

There were eighteen paratroopers in the plane. I wasn't going to jump and sat in the front end of the plane so that I wouldn't be in the way of the jumpers when the time came. The plane was blacked out, but there was no objection to my taking flash pictures once we got over the target. There would be plenty of other kinds of explosions, and my flashbulbs would be just a small part of the show.

We flew low over the Mediterranean and the plane rocked badly. Inside it was dark and silent. Most of the boys were sleeping or maybe just closing their eyes.

Soon I heard peculiar noises. A few of the boys were already beginning to "discover their souls" and were puking violently all over the plane. The boy next to me had been very quiet up to now. But now he turned to me and asked, "Is it true that you're a civilian?"

"Yes," I answered.

He went back inside himself, but in fifteen minutes he asked me again, "You mean to say that if you didn't want to, you didn't have to come?"

"That's right." But silently I added, "If you only knew."

He was quiet again, but this time the interval was shorter. "If you

IN A PLANE EN ROUTE FROM KAIROUAN, TUNISIA, TO SICILY, JULY 1943.
*These American paratroopers are about to launch the Allied invasion
of Sicily.*

had wanted to, could you have flown back to the States tonight instead of this?"

"Not impossible," I said.

Now he was direct. "How much are you getting paid to do this?"

"A thousand a month," I lied.

From then on he didn't have much time to think about my job. The Promised Land emerged from the darkness, well lit by burning houses and flaming oil dumps. Our bombing force had preceded us by half an hour so as to impress the enemy reception committee.

Unfortunately, it hadn't been sufficiently impressed, and the Germans were filling the sky full of colored tracer bullets. Our pilot swerved right and left, trying to find a hole between the tracers.

The green light in the front of our plane came on. It was the signal to get ready to jump. The boys all stood up and straightened the static lines of their parachutes. I got my camera ready. Then the red light came on—the signal to jump. My neighbor was the last one out. He turned back and yelled at me: "I don't like your job, pal. It's too dangerous!" He jumped, and the plane was empty.

I was alone with eighteen broken static lines blowing through the open door. I felt lonelier than hell. I would have given a lot to be with the guys floating down through the darkness below.

—

Chris was waiting for me back at the airfield. He had rigged up a darkroom in a small tent. Under the blacked-out canvas, the heat was suffocating. To keep the developer from boiling, Chris commandeered two huge blocks of ice from the mess sergeant, who protested that they were intended for the next day's ice cream.

We stripped and went to work. Sweat poured down from us into the developing juice. Our first wet prints were ready just as the last hunks of ice melted away. We tore the tent flap open and hit the cool breeze of the desert dawn. Chris had his jeep ready in front of the tent. We threw shirts and trousers on our wet bodies, and Chris drove full speed along the empty road. We headed for Tunis, for a forward press camp, where radio facilities and censors had been set up for the Sicilian show.

While Chris concentrated on the bomb-cratered road, peering

through the semidarkness, I took a look at my pictures. They were slightly out of focus, a bit underexposed, and the composition was certainly no work of art. But they were the only pictures to come out of the invasion of Sicily so far, and it would probably be days before the seaborne photographers managed to send their stuff back from the beaches.

At 7:30 we reached Tunis. The censors, without any argument, stamped my pictures through for radio. We entered the mess room of the press camp just as the loudspeaker was announcing officially that the invasion of Sicily was under way. As the newshounds leaped to their feet at the news, I quietly announced that I'd just returned from there. The only source of first-hand information, I immediately became the center of attraction. I was pressed for details, and I gave a minute-by-minute account of the flight, and described how the invaders' minds and stomachs had behaved from takeoff to jump time.

During the interview, Chris left the mess room. He returned just as I was attacking a pair of fresh eggs. From the doorway, he motioned to me. The eggs were beautiful, but Chris was waving a slip of yellow paper.

Outside, Chris said, "Well, this is it." He gave me the slip, and I read the short message:

PR ALGIERS INFORMED BY COLLIER'S ROBERT CAPA NO LONGER WORK-ING FOR THEM. HE IS ORDERED TO RETURN TO ALGIERS BY FIRST AVAIL-ABLE TRANSPORTATION

I was licked. I had got the pictures, but they would do me no good. The picture pool which had got me fired from *Collier's* would use them with a great splash—without my name—and wouldn't have to pay a single penny for them. "Nuts, I'm going back and eat my eggs," I said.

"Wait a minute," said Chris. "Are you still ready to jump? There's one more mission tonight: we're going to jump the reinforcements in. If you go with them, they won't find you for weeks, and meanwhile I won't acknowledge receipt of the message until tomorrow morning."

So I left my fried eggs and Chris drove me back along the same road, back to the camp where the reinforcements were preparing for the night's work ahead.

—

Chris had no trouble getting me in, and I was given a chute for the asking. At midnight we took off. For the second time in twenty-four hours, I was en route to Sicily. This time I was rigged with the rest of the jumpers, and this time I found my soul like everyone else. All I knew about jumping was that I was supposed to step out of the door with my left foot, count 1,000 … 2,000 … 3,000, and if my chute didn't open, I was to pull the lever for my emergency chute. I was too exhausted to think. I didn't want to think anyway, and I fell asleep.

They woke me up just before the green signal flashed on. When my turn came, I stepped out with my left foot forward into the darkness. I was still groggy, and instead of counting my thousands, I recited: "Fired photographer jumps." I felt a jerk on my shoulder, and my chute was open. "Fired photographer floats," I said happily to myself. Less than a minute later, I landed in a tree in the middle of a forest.

For the rest of the night, I hung from the tree, and my shoulders found out the weight of my behind. The general was right, it wasn't natural. There was a lot of shooting going on around me. I didn't dare yell for help. With my Hungarian accent, I stood an equal chance of being shot by either side.

When morning came, three paratroopers discovered me and cut me down. I said good-bye to my tree. Our relations had been intimate, but a little too long.

—

Our four-man task force wasn't eager to engage the enemy, and we advanced cautiously from tree to tree, and only after long deliberation. As the forest thinned out, our confabs grew longer. From behind the last tree, we saw a little Sicilian farmhouse. It was out in the open field some two hundred yards away. In the best military fashion, we crawled up to the house on our stomachs. The three soldiers surrounded the house and occupied strategic positions, ready to fire with their tommy guns. Having no tommy gun, and being the linguist of the group, I was given the job of knocking on the door.

AGRIGENTO, SICILY, JULY 17–18, 1943. *Life resumes in the liberated, but badly damaged, city.*

An old Sicilian peasant in a long nightshirt opened the door. He looked at me as if I had dropped from the sky. My jumpsuit was a new uniform to him. We all wore American flags as shoulder patches, but my dark, slightly Mediterranean face must have impressed him more than anything, for he suddenly screamed, *"Siciliano! Siciliano!"* and threw his arms around me. My army lowered their tommy guns and we quickly entered the farmhouse. I didn't know any Italian, so in broken Spanish I tried to explain to the old man that only my great grandfather was Sicilian. He answered with a stream of strange words. There was one word he kept repeating, "Brook-a-leen." One of my troopers caught on and pointed to himself. "Me, Brooklyn."

The conversation became easier and we established that Americans like Sicilians and Sicilians love Americans; that Americans don't like Germans and Sicilians hate Germans. These preliminaries over, I came to the point. Where were we, and were any Germans around?

We laid our silk invasion map on the table. The Sicilian peasant, after first admiring the quality of the fabric, put his thumb on a point way inland, some twenty-five miles beyond our official dropping zone. Some German units had passed on the road leading to the coast during the night, he said, but they hadn't stopped and he didn't think there were any more around.

He gave us food and wine and we returned to the forest. We remained there for three days, sleeping in the daytime and creeping out at night to blow up little bridges. On the fourth day, the spearhead of the 1st Division caught up with us. They were not terribly impressed with our military prowess, and as for the photographer—the whole bloody thing had been absolutely useless to me. The only picture I had was a portrait of the old Sicilian farmer.

———

The Sicilian campaign turned out to be a twenty-one-day race. In the lead was the Italian Army. They were afraid not only of the Americans, but of the Germans too, and ran in every direction. The Germans were slower than the Italians, but they retreated steadily. Close on their heels came the jobless enemy alien, who in turn was chased by the whole public relations force of the American Army.

Behind us all, pushing us relentlessly forward, General Patton's tanks rumbled in the dust.

In the course of things, I shot a great many exciting pictures. But the only way to get them censored and shipped was through the very P.R.O. from which I was running. Besides, the only place I could ship them was the picture pool, and that wouldn't help me a bit. The exposed rolls piled up in my bag and the chances of getting them published dwindled every day.

In less than three weeks we reached our main objective. We were at the outskirts of Palermo. The Germans had withdrawn, and the remaining Italian forces didn't insist on fighting. The jeep I was in followed the first tanks of the 2d Armored Division into the town. The road leading into the city was lined with tens of thousands of frantic Sicilians waving white sheets and homemade American flags with not enough stars and too many stripes. Everyone had a cousin in Brook-a-leen.

I was unanimously pronounced a Siciliano by the cheering crowd. Every member of the male population had to shake my hand, the older women had to kiss me, the younger ones filled the jeep with flowers and fruit. None of this exactly helped my picture taking.

We arrived at the gates of Palermo without firing a shot. The lieutenant in charge of the tanks got in touch with headquarters by radio and asked for orders to enter the city. When headquarters found that there was no resistance in the town, they ordered us to stop and wait for the commanding general. We called headquarters unprintable names and waited. In a short while, the corps commander, General Keyes, arrived surrounded by aides and swarms of military police. The MP's promptly took over and blocked off any further advance by tanks, soldiers, or war correspondents.

General Keyes ordered the MP's to bring forward a few of the celebrating Italian gendarmes. The gendarmes were produced. General Keyes said he didn't give a damn about their innocence; all he wanted was the Italian general in command of Palermo. The gendarmes nodded and said, "Yes, yes," but did not move. The exasperated Keyes asked for an interpreter and I offered my services. I got the point over to the gendarmes somehow. I explained that the gen-

MONREALE, ON THE OUTSKIRTS OF PALERMO, SICILY, JULY 1943. *Welcoming the American troops.*

PALERMO, SICILY, JULY 1943. *General Giuseppe Molinero (right), the commanding officer of Palermo, surrenders the city to General Geoffrey Keyes of the U.S. Army.*

Overleaf:
MONREALE, ON THE OUTSKIRTS OF
PALERMO, SICILY, JULY 1943.
American troops enter the city.

PALERMO, SICILY, JULY 1943. *Americans enjoying victory.*

SICILY, JULY 1943. *An injured American soldier.*

eral wanted to avoid any unnecessary bloodshed and wanted the Italian general to announce the terms of surrender to the populace. The gendarmes nodded *"Si, si,"* climbed into a jeep with a couple of MP's, and took off toward the center of town.

In fifteen minutes the jeep reappeared. Seated in the back, between the two beaming gendarmes, was a very unhappy Italian major general. General Keyes motioned the sweating Italian general into his command car and repeated his order to the MP's not to let anyone through. He had a white flag hoisted on his car and it looked as if he was going to take Palermo without the Army.

Here goes my surrender ceremony, I thought. But just as the car was about to leave, General Keyes turned toward me. "Interpreter, come along," he ordered.

We drove up to the governor's palace and dismounted in the courtyard. General Keyes demanded the immediate and unconditional surrender of the town and military district of Palermo. I translated it into French, the language I knew best, and hoped the Italian would understand me. He replied in perfect French and said that he would be only too glad to do so, but it was really impossible. He had already surrendered four hours earlier to an American infantry division that had entered the city from the opposite direction.

General Keyes became impatient at the delay. "Stop that jabbering, soldier! I want unconditional surrender and I want it immediately!"

I explained to the Italian that surrendering the second time ought to be much easier than the first. Besides, General Keyes was the corps commander, and would undoubtedly allow him to keep his orderly and personal belongings in the prisoners' camp. The issue was won. He surrendered in French, Italian, and Sicilian, and asked whether he could keep his wife too.

My translator's job was done, and I went back to taking pictures. Later, when the surrender ceremony was over, I saw the Italian general being led away to prison—empty-handed and alone.

The Army poured into Palermo. Ernie Pyle was riding in the first press jeep. He waved at me and shouted:

NEAR TROINA, SICILY, AUGUST 4–5, 1943. *A Sicilian peasant tells an American officer which way the Germans had gone.*

"You goddamn fired enemy alien, the whole PR is after you!"

There would be no victory celebration in Palermo for me. I turned over my films to Ernie and asked him to ship them to *Life* magazine. By now, either they had decided to hire me, or—if not— once they saw these pictures, they couldn't help but do so.

I had to leave Palermo, and on foot. Leaving all the promised pleasures of our first occupied capital, I was sick and tired of being a fired photographer. I had no idea where to go, but I knew that the 1st Division was fighting somewhere in the middle of Sicily. I had chums there, and decided to join them. I didn't know exactly where they were, and it took me three long days to find them. The two commanding generals, Terry Allen and Teddy Roosevelt, were friends of mine, but division headquarters was hardly safe for me. By now, everyone knew that I had no right to pose as an accredited war photographer. So I carefully avoided headquarters and fell in with the 16th Infantry Regiment, the same group that had once been my family in North Africa.

The regiment was just jumping off to take Troina, a small town perched on a hilltop. Troina was tough. It took us seven days to capture it and we lost a lot of good men.

This was the first time I had followed an attack from beginning to end, and I managed to get some good pictures. They were simple pictures and showed how dreary and unspectacular fighting actually is. Scoops depend on luck and quick transmission, and most of them don't mean anything the day after they are published. But the soldier who looks at the shots of Troina, ten years from now in his home in Ohio, will be able to say, "That's how it was."

The lovely little mountain village was in ruins. The Germans who had been defending it had pulled out during the night, and had left the dead and wounded Italian civilians behind. We were lying around in the little square in front of the church, completely pooped and thoroughly disgusted. There wasn't much sense to this fighting, dying, taking pictures, I was thinking, when Teddy Roosevelt, who always showed up where the fighting was roughest, drove up. He poked at me with his stick, and said, "Capa, there's a message down at division headquarters saying you're working for *Life*."

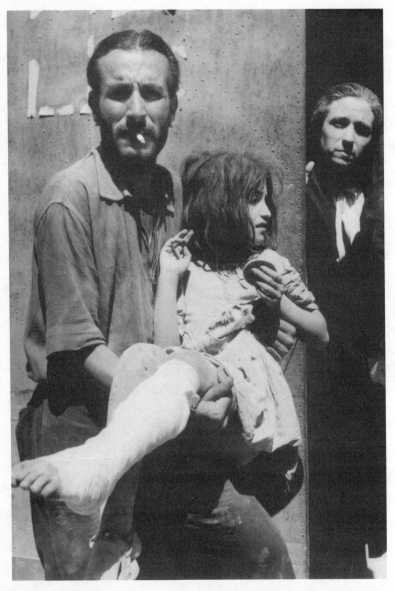

TROINA, SICILY, AUGUST 6, 1943. *American forces bombed and shelled this hilltop German stronghold for a week. Some Italian civilians had been trapped in the town, as Capa discovered upon his entry into Troina with the first American patrol.*

TROINA, SICILY, AUGUST 1943.

TROINA, SICILY, AUGUST 1943.

I had hoped and prayed for this news for a long time. But now that it had come, I wasn't really happy. I felt that the jobless enemy alien I was leaving behind in Troina was much more a part of this war than the fully accredited *Life* photographer ever could be.

———

The prodigal returned to Palermo by jeep. During the ride, General Teddy recited poetry and Lieutenant Stevenson sang cowboy songs. I was feeling a bit dizzy. We stopped for chow, but I couldn't eat. My companions remarked that I looked a little on the green side. There was no doubt of it, I had got the job and malaria both at the same time.

The hospital had bad food and a good-looking nurse. I couldn't eat the food, and the doctor asked the nurse to give me a couple of shots of Scotch every day in order to help my appetite. The nurse brought me a pile of American newspapers, and I discovered that my pictures of the invasion of Sicily had been used by every paper in the States. They didn't mention my name, but *Life* made up for it. They carried my story of the entry of Palermo as a seven-page lead article. There was not only a fat byline, but also my face in a little box. It said that I was a staff photographer.

I asked the nurse whether there was any good food to be found in Palermo. There was a pretty good black-market restaurant in the Hotel Excelsior, she said. She felt my pulse, said that I was still running a temperature, and that we could get out unnoticed through the basement window after dark.

We had nice steaks and drank spumanti. We had a very good time. When we got back to the hospital it was quite late and the window was locked.

I behaved like an eighteenth-century gallant, sent the nurse to her quarters, walked in the main entrance, and said that I was a new patient. I thought I had a touch of malaria, I added. They admitted me all over again. Unfortunately, I was sent to the same ward, and it was the same doctor who came to look me over. This time I got fired from the hospital.

VII

The Sicilian campaign was over, and I was shipped back to Algiers. The main press headquarters was bustling with activity, and in the briefing room—where the official handout was usually read to a handful of press agency men—I found an impressive gallery of well-known byliners. The speedy conquest of Sicily together with the impending invasion of the mainland of Europe had brought them tearing over from their desks in America in one hell of a hurry.

The room was buzzing with speculation as to when and where the Big Thing would take place. Talk about airpower, soft underbellies, and extended supply lines filled the air, but it failed to impress my quinine-stuffed head, and I decided to beat it. I wanted a room to myself with a great big bed. I wanted a bathtub and fresh towels, and a buzzer to summon a waiter.

There were only two large hotels in Algiers. On the hilltop was the St. George, which served as Eisenhower's military headquarters. The second was the Aletti, overlooking the harbor. It was reserved for visiting generals from the front, for diplomats and war correspondents, for important Free French and the still important Vichy French, and for very high-class ladies of dubious occupation.

When I reached the Aletti, the billeting sergeant gave me—

instead of a room key—a well-rehearsed little speech. In November of 1942, he said, there were only twenty-two accredited war correspondents in Algiers, and the town major had allotted them ten rooms in the hotel. Now, however, in August of 1943, there were about a hundred and fifty accredited correspondents, and still the same ten rooms. I started to argue with him. He answered with a shrug. The rooms were on the third floor, he said, and I could try my luck.

My chances of getting a bed to myself had vanished, but I still had hopes for the tub and the buzzer. I went from room to room, asking to share a bed, pleading for a share of the floor space, but all in vain. Not only was every bed occupied, but every square foot of floor space was covered with a cot or a bedroll, all crowded side by side. Even the few balconies had been commandeered.

I parked myself and my bedroll in an empty corner in the lobby, and sat lost in dejection. At this point, the 230-pound hulk of my old boss Quentin Reynolds turned up. He was glad to hear that I had gotten a job, and told me not to worry about a room. Coming over from England, he had made friends with a meek little man representing something called the British Council. The B.C. must have been quite important, because the little man had been given a room with two beds and a balcony all for himself. Quent was using the second bed, and was quite sure that his little friend wouldn't object to a friendly Hungarian taking up a small part of the floor.

That night, when the little man came home, he discovered me stretched on his floor. He apologized for waking me, and hoped I was quite comfortable. I mumbled that I was and went back to sleep instantly.

Next morning, we were awakened by Clark Lee, the handsomest of all foreign correspondents, who was as famous for his reporting as for his escape from Bataan. He was slightly less handsome that morning, his face swollen by a badly infected tooth. He pointed with one hand to his face, with the other to the bed. The meek little B.C. gentleman obligingly got out, and the moaning Clark crawled in.

In the evening, the B.C. man retrieved his bed. Just as we were getting settled, the door opened and Jack Belden, the sweetest and also sourest tempered of the correspondents, walked in. He silently undid his bedroll, and crawled in to sleep. We felt that our host had a word of explanation coming, and offered that Jack had been with Stilwell in the retreat from Burma.

Ernie Pyle came in around midnight. He was the shyest of men. All the rest of us were rather big fellows, he apologized, but his slim presence would hardly be noticed.

That seemed plenty for one night, but we were due to be awakened once more. The visitors this time were a dozen German planes, flying low, and dropping their bombs a few hundred yards from our window. We stayed where we were, but put on our helmets. The gentleman of the B.C. had no helmet, however, and decided he would feel safer under the bed. Clark Lee didn't mind, and for the rest of the night he was back in a bed again.

The next day we were still waiting for a call from Public Relations. We sat around the room a bit bored, just a bit scared, and chewed the fat about the Big Move. John Steinbeck and H. R. "Red" Knickerbocker dropped in along about afternoon, with three bottles of Algerian schnapps. They thought it would help Clark Lee's headache, they said. The stuff tasted like hell, but we couldn't see Clark drink it by himself. So we pitched in and helped empty the bottles before the awful stuff could kill him. In the meanwhile, Steinbeck and Knickerbocker were quietly undoing their bedrolls out on the balcony.

From then on, each morning found some new addition to our ménage. From the balcony, we could see the harbor clearly. Every day more and more ships were loaded with troops, guns, and planes. The empty spaces between the large ships were gradually filled with dozens of small invasion barges. The Big When was coming closer.

Just about the time when there was no longer any space to walk between the bodies in our room, we got our call to report to headquarters. We packed our helmets and our bedrolls, bid farewell to our little host, and left him sad and all alone in the empty room.

———

We piled into PR headquarters. Lieutenant Colonel Joe Phillips, the head PR, called us into his office one by one. We were told nothing about the operation, only that from now on we would be "isolated." One by one, we were assigned to our divisions. When my turn came, Phillips said, "Capa, I'm convinced that you're a born paratrooper." I protested that I was a born Hungarian. He laughed. "I think we'd better stick to the first version."

A few hours later, I was delivered to the airfield at Kairouan. I had been there about six weeks earlier, and the planes and gliders were lined up in exactly the same formation as before. Now, however, there were little white parachutes painted on the noses of the C-47's—one parachute for each mission over enemy territory.

Chris was expecting me, and greeted me on my arrival. "Congratulations. I hear you got the job and you're fully legal. How is Pinky?"

I answered that I had no troubles of any kind. He was disappointed. "You're just as boring as any other newspaperman," he said. "But I have news for you. Si Korman of the *Chicago Tribune* is here, and his poker is even worse than yours."

I played just as badly as ever, but by midnight I had everyone's money. Getting up from the table, Chris complained about my exceptional luck. There could be only one explanation, he said. Pinky was having a good time.

The following day, Chris had to fly over to Cairo. I gave him the poker money and asked him to buy me five pairs of silk stockings and a bottle of the best French perfume. He accepted the commission, but didn't think it would help me.

Thirty-six hours later, Chris was back with the stuff. I sent it off to Pinky with a note. Before the stockings were gone, I promised, I would be back in London.

The days passed slowly in the hot Tunisian desert. There was still no sign of D-Day. The 82d Airborne and 9th Troop Carrier headquarters were enveloped in top secrecy and the planning rooms were barred to unclassified personnel.

We were tired of waiting in the sun and were impatient for the day we would be told to jump. Finally the day came—but instead of boarding our planes, we were ordered aboard a lot of LCI's that were waiting in nearby Gafsa harbor.

For two days we zigzagged up and down the Mediterranean. Then we abruptly changed course and landed in the harbor of Licata, in Sicily. The jump was on again, and the planes of the 9th TCC had already been transferred from Kairouan to the Licata airfield.

Chris was there too, and had a pressroom ready for us. The big brass had taken over the Licata high school, and the PR was established in the laboratory. Surrounded by glass beakers, skeletons, and stuffed birds, Dick Tregaskis, of the INS, typed glowing preinvasion stories which never passed the censor, and Korman and I played two-handed poker on a tilted blackboard.

The airborne division, alerted for action, camped in an olive grove just behind the Licata airfield. Licata, the town made famous by John Hersey in his book *A Bell for Adano,* did not yet have a bell, but there was plenty of fish and sour wine. The evening was cool in the open camp, the sky full of stars and mosquitoes, and fresh rumors circulated freely under the olive trees.

The next morning, Brigadier General Taylor, of the 82d Airborne, asked if anyone could lend him a money belt. I remembered the story told about General Mark Clark, who had arrived secretly on the coast of North Africa to prepare the way for the African invasion. Surprised by gendarmes as he landed on the beach, he had lost both his trousers and millions of francs of bribe money in the ensuing scuffle.

I offered General Taylor the money belt which I had acquired with the change in my poker luck, and asked him if he intended losing only his trousers.

The general took my belt with the comment that newspapermen talk too much.

Two days later, the camp broke into feverish activity. We were ordered to check our equipment and pack our things. I was asked to report to General Ridgway, the commanding general, at his tent.

"Capa," he said to me, "you're going to have dinner in Rome tonight. General Taylor is there now, and the armistice with the Italians has been signed."

Our airborne troops were going to occupy both the airfield and the city of Rome that night. "Marshal Badoglio has assured us he

will have the airfield free from the Germans, secure for our landing."
He went on to explain that the Fifth Army would land at Salerno,
south of Naples, the following morning.

This would be one of the big scoops of the war. While the rest of
the photographers were taking pictures of a dreary beach and
maybe a few local mayors, I would catch Mussolini at home. And by
the time my colleagues reached Rome, I would be firmly established
in the best hotel in Italy, calling the bartender by his first name.

I returned to my bedroll and changed from my jumpsuit to a pair
of pink trousers and a gabardine shirt. A little while later I was sitting in General Ridgway's lead plane, ready for the takeoff.

Our motors were warming up when a messenger ran up and
handed the general a radio message. It was from General Taylor in
Rome:

GERMANS OCCUPIED AIRFIELD THIS AFTERNOON ITALIANS UNABLE TO
STOP THEM ADVISE CANCELING ALL PLANS

I was the saddest guy in pink trousers in all Italy.

———

Three days after the Fifth Army had landed at Salerno, a boat carrying the three airborne correspondents dropped anchor at that
fateful harbor. It had been only seventy-two hours, but for some
guys it had been the longest seventy-two hours of their lives—for
many, their last. The charred, half-submerged hulls of ships and
barges, the flags waving over the white crosses of the first American
cemetery on the European mainland—all this told us what Salerno
had been.

A "Duck" took us from the boat to the beach, and after five years'
absence I was back in Europe. Something new had been added by
courtesy of the Fifth Army. Big signs split up the beach into Red,
Green, and Yellow landing areas; the newly built roads were identified as Main Street, Broadway, and 42nd Street; MP's in spotless
white gloves were directing traffic at the intersections; and each corner was decorated with extra-big signs on which were inscribed the
Ten Commandments of the Fifth:

SOLDIERS NOT WEARING THEIR HELMETS WILL BE FINED. SALUTING OF OFFICERS WILL BE STRICTLY ENFORCED. JEEPS MAY BE DRIVEN ONLY BY THOSE HOLDING SPECIALLY AUTHORIZED TRIP TICKETS.

The press camp was established in a factory about a mile inland, and we had to show all kinds of identification to be admitted to the sacred area. All the correspondents were there and every one of them had already sent in two or three of the most sensational stories of the war.

We looked at the situation map. The front was only four to six miles inland, and our most forward position was still twenty miles short of Naples. On the left flank of the beachhead, the one closest to Naples and also farthest from headquarters, was a blue square reading: Rangers, Commandos, and Paratroopers.

Having missed the invasion story, I wanted to be with the outfit that had the best chance of reaching Naples first. So I set out in the direction of Maiori, where the Rangers had their headquarters.

The Rangers may not have been better than any of the good infantry regiments, but most of them had gotten tougher training and more experience. They talked like jerks, fought like killers—and once I found them crying like heroes. As for their commander, Lieutenant Colonel Darby, he talked tougher and fought rougher than any of them.

I arrived in Maiori that evening. I was good and tired and decided to look for a bed. The best place to find food and a bed at the beginning of any invasion is always a hospital. I found the hospital in a little church. It wasn't hard to find: a long line of ambulances were making a steady procession toward it.

At the entrance to the church, the ambulances were disgorging their blood-covered stretchers. In the dark interior, the moaning of the wounded made a strange kind of prayer, and the smell of ether blended with that of incense. The church was full. Most of the wounded had to lie on the cold floor. There were only a few army cots, and they had been assigned to the hopelessly wounded. Over their heads, like sacristy lamps, hung plasma bottles, and the trickling blood tried to catch their escaping lives.

Before the altar, kneeling alone, his back to the congregation of wounded and dying, his face pressed to the steps, was a soldier who seemed to be their priest. He had no wounds I could see, but a shell had exploded near him and had shattered his nerves and blown the senses out of his body. He mumbled a steady stream of incoherent sounds, and only God knew what he said.

Italian nuns were looking after the wounded, and the first German prisoners were scrubbing the floor. I hesitated, then I brought out my camera. My flashbulb mercilessly broke the spell. I was a photographer, this was an unusual hospital... it made a good story.

The doctors' quarters were in the orphanage adjoining the church. The doctor in charge gave me his bed. He had no time to use it himself.

We had breakfast together in the morning, the doctor and I. While we ate, the orphans marched out into the church garden in close formation, led by the mother superior. They were singing songs and they were the songs of the young Fascisti. The doctor had been falling asleep over his coffee, but he became suddenly alert and shouted for the interpreter.

"You can tell the mother superior that we're not going to have this sort of thing anymore. I refuse to nourish any future fascists on American rations. If these kids don't break formation and learn to play like normal kids, there won't be any food at lunchtime."

There was a long argument, with the mother superior finally stalking out of the building. The children started to behave like wild Indians—and the new democracy was born.

For a moment, the doctor relaxed and smiled. Then his face grew serious again, he got up abruptly, and hurried back to his operating room.

———

At Ranger headquarters, I found Lieutenant Colonel Darby and his small staff at breakfast. They were unshaven and unslept for days, and the colonel was trying to answer three telephones at the same time.

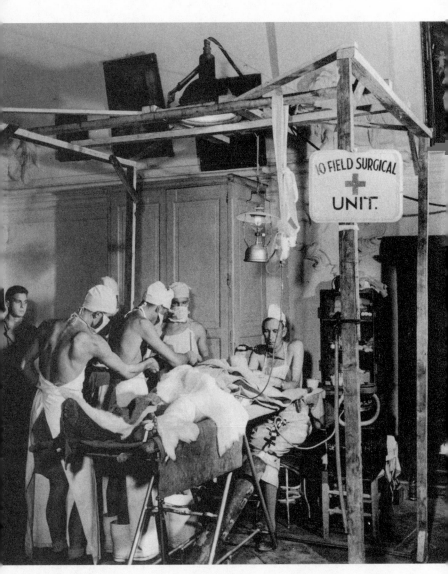

MAIORI (SORRENTO PENINSULA), SEPTEMBER 19, 1943. *A British surgical unit works in an operating room set up in a church in the northern sector of the Salerno beachhead.*

"What can I do for you, photographer?" he asked.

I told him I was in a hurry to catch up with the war.

That shouldn't be hard, he answered. He hadn't many troops, even less matériel, but plenty of war, and he could spare a little for me. His front was the entire left flank of the beachhead; his army included, besides the Rangers, a regiment of paratroopers, a battalion of the 36th Infantry Division, a few British commandos, and a task force of light British tanks; he had a few pieces of artillery, two mortar companies, and a British light cruiser anchored in the bay.

"If you insist on getting shot at, the Chiunzi Pass is as good a place as any. Stick around a bit, my driver will take you up to Fort Schuster."

On both sides of the narrow, winding mountain road were vineyards, and the ripe blue grapes were warm and beautiful. I suggested to the driver that we stop for a moment. Instead of slowing down, he stepped on the gas. He pointed to the new craters and to a GI lying flat in a ditch along the road.

"I'm not stopping," he said. "Not on this bloody road."

A shell whistled. It exploded only a hundred yards behind us. I was convinced. The grapes were probably sour anyway.

———

Fort Schuster turned out to be an old Italian tavern built in the deep curve of the road on top of the pass. The tavern was hundreds of years old and had thick walls made of native stone. On the other side of the curve, the road slid down to the flat plain of Naples, but it was days before I dared step outside to admire the view.

Fort Schuster was a first-aid station, and had been named for the doctor in charge. There was a large table in the middle of the room that was used for emergency operations. When I entered, the medics were preparing some wounded for the trip down to the church in Maiori.

I had been taking pictures of war and blood since Spain, but even after seven years the sight of torn flesh and fresh blood brought my stomach up close behind my eyes. I parked my bedroll in the farthest corner, beside two enormous barrels of wine.

The Germans were shelling the pass and the ridge without a

letup. The shells exploded all around us, but the tavern was protected by the curve of the sunken road, and was a difficult target to hit.

The boys in the foxholes on the ridge, however, were getting it badly, and by midnight the tavern was full. Near the door, the dead; in the center, the wounded; and in the far corner—the barrels and the photographer.

During the night Lieutenant Colonel Walker, commander of the infantry battalion of the 36th Division, appeared with his staff. "Sorry, doc, but we have to move in. The Germans have opened up with two new mortar batteries, and they've zeroed-in on my command post."

They set up their telephones amid the wounded. The place was so crowded that I moved my bedroll into the hollow under the two enormous barrels.

Later, a mortar shell exploded right at the entrance to the pass and some of the shrapnel broke through the mattresses that covered the windows. Under the additional protection of a hundred and fifty gallons of wine, I felt relatively safe.

The shelling continued all night. The Germans had got the exact range of our positions on the ridge and our companies sent in new casualty reports after every explosion. Lieutenant Colonel Walker, reporting to Ranger headquarters, said that his observers hadn't been able to locate the new enemy mortars. He was afraid his rapidly dwindling battalion wouldn't be able to hold.

Darby ordered him to hold at any price, and he'd get reinforcements to us by daylight. At dawn, the reinforcements arrived. They consisted of a 75-millimeter gun mounted on a battered half-track, manned by four Rangers. On the armor plate of the half-track were painted the names of four famous battles: Oran, Kasserine Pass, Hill 609, and Gela Beach. Captain O'Brien was in command. He wore a

Overleaf: CHIUNZI PASS, ABOVE MAIORI (SORRENTO PENINSULA), SEPTEMBER 1943. *Foxholes outside the strategic outpost that the Americans called "Fort Schuster," overlooking the main road leading north to Naples.*

Silver Star on his shirt and a luxuriant mustache on his lip. He hoped it made him look older than his twenty-one years.

Our faces fell. One light gun against two German mortar batteries! O'Brien enjoyed our discomfort for a moment; then, to our relief, he told us that a lot of powerful stuff was on its way.

O'Brien's mission was to find those evasive German mortars, and he offered us a simple plan. He would move his truck about seventy-five yards out into the open. The Germans would open fire on him and thereby show their positions. It was a bold idea and sure to draw all the fire right onto the pass, but Walker had no choice and told him to go ahead.

I chose the camera that had the longest lens. I wanted to be able to photograph the entire action from the door of the fort. The half-track moved out. Soon the whistles of the incoming and outgoing shells couldn't be told apart. I had to jump back into the tavern between shots, but I was able to get thirty-six pictures of the spectacular show.

In about twelve minutes the half-track had exhausted all its ammunition, and it moved back into the pass. O'Brien and his crew were unhurt, but the truck bore fresh dents. They were sure that the fire was coming from the little village in the woods just below the pass and a patrol was sent out to investigate. The shells kept coming, the plaster kept falling, but all we could do was wait.

At dusk, a young American lieutenant arrived with four heavy mortars. With him was a young British lieutenant with a little radio and two men. The British chap represented the cruiser that was anchored in the bay.

The mortars were set up in our backyard. The cruiser stood by, ready to fire at any target we should radio them.

The patrol returned a short while later and reported that the German mortars were located in the village. The guns were cleverly hidden in various farmhouses and were firing their mortars through big holes that had been cut in the roofs.

We made plans to give a little demonstration of the combined artillery of the Allied powers as soon as it became light. First, the chemical company would fire smoke shells from their four mortars.

"FORT SCHUSTER," SEPTEMBER 1943. *American lookouts radio observations to a British cruiser offshore that is shelling the Axis forces in the villages below the Chiunzi Pass.*

"FORT SCHUSTER," SEPTEMBER 1943. *Time for grub.*

Then, the British cruiser would pour in the Empire's contribution from its eight guns. And last, the half-track would move out again and shoot at any Germans who tried to run from the village. As for me, I would sneak out during the night, find myself a well-covered place overlooking the village, and would shoot everything with my camera.

I spent half the night clinging to the mountainside. I was violently homesick for Fort Schuster and felt that I deserved a raise.

The first rays of the rising sun lit up my stage. The village was only 750 yards below me, set against the backdrop of Vesuvius, which was pouring out a beautiful, thick column of smoke. I envied Vesuvius. I couldn't even light a cigarette for fear I'd give my hiding place away.

The plain was stiller than a cemetery on a Wednesday afternoon. I could distinguish clearly the hundreds of farmhouses situated among the vineyards, and felt that I could be distinguished just as clearly from there. Every window looked straight into my eyes, and I tried to scrunch even lower into my bush. My behind was cold and I hated the beautiful view. All I wanted to see were the dirty walls of Fort Schuster, and I wanted to see them from the inside. Here, lying flat as a pancake on the cold ground between the two lines, I had only two alternatives: to be scared on my stomach, or scared on my back.

Our first smoke shell landed squarely in the center of the village. The mortars, the cruiser, and the half-track proceeded to pour hundreds of shells into the white smoke. I lifted my head no more than three inches from the ground and took my pictures. But it was always the same picture. All I could do was use a different color filter for each shot. The smoke from the village rose to the sky. Vesuvius, in the background, looked like a kid brother.

The shells went straight over my head, the mortars whistled, the cruiser screamed, and the half-track added a high dissonant squeak. Then the German shells answered back, whining and hitting the hilltop just a hundred yards above me. I buried my head in the foliage. The sun was warming my back, and I wished that it was only birds that were flying and singing in the air.

It was all quiet again by sundown. A thin film of black smoke still rose to the sky from the burning walls of the village houses, and Vesuvius—undisturbed—puffed away as usual.

I crawled back to Fort Schuster in the dark, and found that Major General Ridgway and Colonel Darby had taken over. The 82d Airborne had been brought up to Maiori and the final attack on Naples was set for the following morning.

I packed my bedroll and said good-bye to Fort Schuster. At midnight, I crossed the Chiunzi Pass behind a brigade of British armor, and by daylight we were down in the plain. The Germans had retreated during the night. The little houses, which had so scared me, were filled with celebrating Italians. They offered us fruit, wine, and the eternal chatter about their waiting for us all their lives.

—

We met no resistance along the way and stopped only to inquire whether the road ahead was safe, take a swig of wine, or maybe kiss a girl. At Pompeii, one of the GI's started raving about the dirty pictures on the walls of the ancient ruins. So we dismounted and, led by two old Italian tourist guides, saw the ruins for a fee of two lire each. The beautiful frescoes, which told of the art of Roman lovemaking, were easily understood and greatly appreciated by the invaders. We tipped the guides and were off again to Naples.

The new ruins of Naples had painted on them something different. In large letters, the walls read MORE IL FASCISMO and VIVE LOS AMERICANOS. The girls looked very dirty—the reservoir in Naples had been cut off about four weeks before.

Taking pictures of victory is like taking pictures of a church wedding ten minutes after the departure of the newlyweds. The ceremony in Naples had been very brief. Some confetti still glittered among the filth of the place, but the empty-stomached merrymakers had quickly dispersed, already wondering how much the bride and groom would quarrel the next day. With my cameras hanging around my neck, I walked along the deserted streets, unhappy and yet glad that I had such a good excuse for not taking more pictures. When I got back to the Hotel Parco, where I was staying, I would have a clear conscience and a natural thirst.

The narrow street leading to my hotel was blocked by a queue of silent people in front of a schoolhouse. It was not a food line because the people coming out of the building held only their hats in their hands. I fell in behind the queue. I entered the school and was met by the sweet, sickly smell of flowers and the dead. In the room were twenty primitive coffins, not well enough covered with flowers and too small to hide the dirty little feet of children—children old enough to fight the Germans and be killed, but just a little too old to fit in children's coffins.

These children of Naples had stolen rifles and bullets and had fought the Germans for fourteen days, while we had been pinned to the Chiunzi Pass. These children's feet were my real welcome to Europe, I who had been born there. More real by far than the welcome of the hysterically cheering crowds I had met along the road, many of them the same that had yelled *Duce!* in an earlier year.

I took off my hat and got out my camera. I pointed the lens at the faces of the prostrated women, taking little pictures of their dead babies, until finally the coffins were carried away. Those were my truest pictures of victory, the ones I took at that simple schoolhouse funeral.

———

I soon found other pictures of victory. Back at my hotel, General Clark's public relations officer was waiting to take me to an important ceremony. The important ceremony was to take place in the Royal Gardens, where the Fifth Army had set up provisional headquarters. The general's trailer was parked under the big oak trees and a number of full "chicken" colonels were running around arranging chairs. One of the colonels advised me to take my pictures of the general from the side where I could see the stars on his cap. The general, with his three shiny stars, soon arrived. So did the Bishop of Naples, with beautiful, shiny ornaments dangling from his purple robe.

I took position as commanded, to port of the general. The general was a gracious and happy victor. As for the bishop, he had been practicing for three years—with different German generals—for this very occasion. They beamed at each other and shook hands for such a long while that even the slowest photographer could not miss.

NAPLES, OCTOBER 2, 1943. *Funeral for twenty teenage partisans at the Liceo Sannazaro in the Vómero district.*

NAPLES, OCTOBER 2, 1943. *The mothers and other relatives of the fallen partisans.*

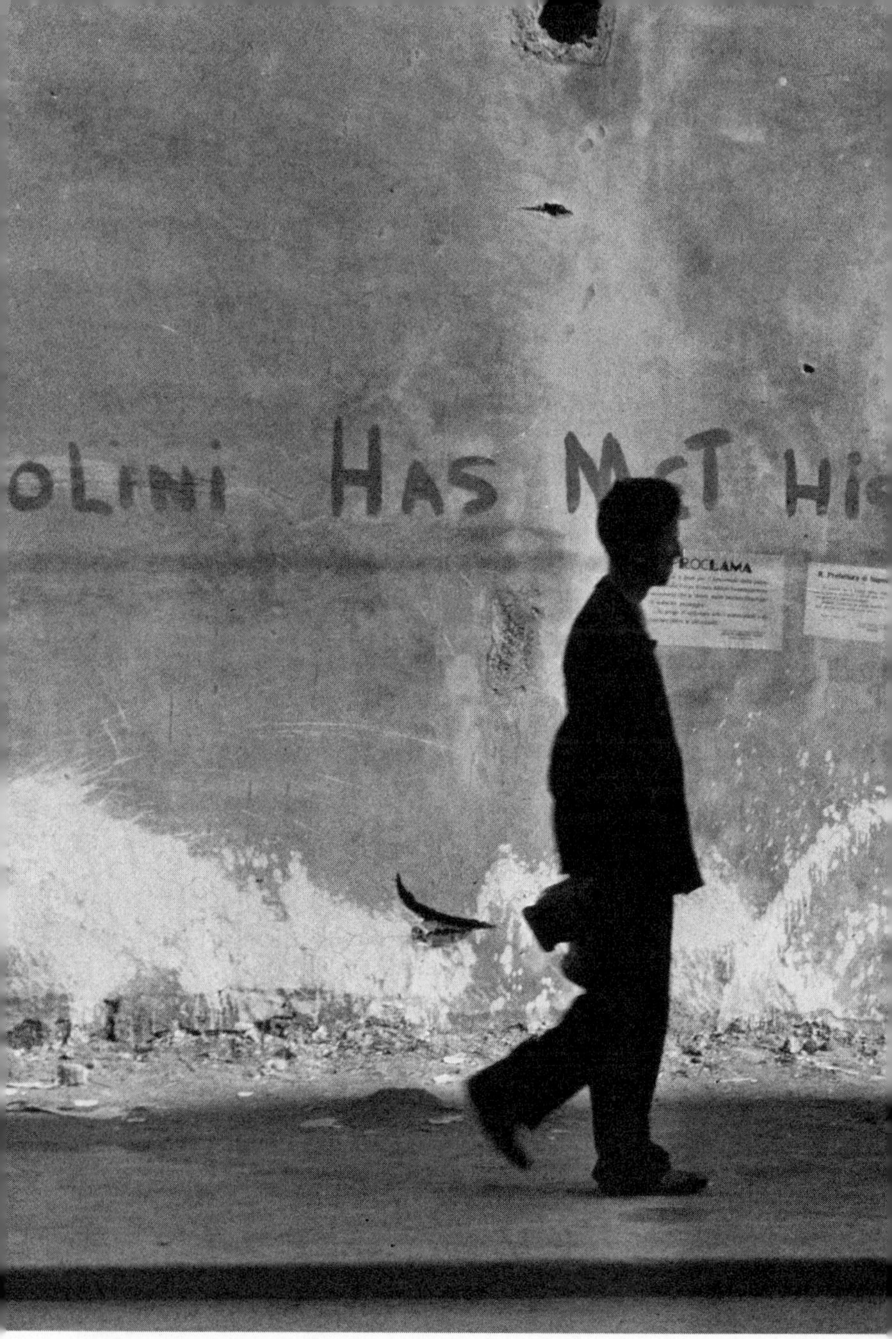
OLINI HAS MET HI
ROCLAMA

NAPLES, OCTOBER 1943.

NAPLES, OCTOBER 7, 1943. *Before they abandoned the city, the Germans planted a massive time bomb in the basement of the Central Post Office. It went off a week later, killing a hundred people and injuring many more.*

NAPLES, OCTOBER 1943. *On their retreat northward, the Germans had dynamited the city's water supply system. Therefore, the citizens had to obtain water from Allied tank trucks.*

I prepared my shipment for *Life*, and sent the films of the dead children and those of the general's reception in the same envelope.

———

Victory was boring, and the dirty streets of hungry Naples soon walked on my nerves. My thirtieth birthday was coming up and I decided to celebrate it in comfort. The Isle of Capri, which was completely untouched by war, was only five miles away, and had just been designated as a rest center for the American air force. Moreover, Chris arrived in Naples, and thought that this first rest camp in Italy could well use a visit from an expert public relations officer.

Capri received us as if we were pigeons heralding the return of the Anglo-Saxon tourist trade. We got no rest. During the day, the whole hotel staff feverishly practiced their half-forgotten English on us. At night, every available guitar serenaded us from beneath our hotel window. They played one song in particular over and over again. It sounded strangely familiar, and I bet Chris five dollars that the song was "Happy Days Are Here Again."

Around midnight we went down to find out. No, they said, it was "Happy Birthday to You." Chris used the fiver to get rid of the musicians, and I was thirty years old.

———

The next morning, the president of the newly formed Union of Anti-Fascist Tourist Guides rowed us all around the island and showed us the famous blue and green grottoes. In addition, he gave us a detailed list of collaborators and urged us to have them arrested immediately upon our return. In the afternoon, the president of the Collaborators' Association presented us with a case of old brandy. We accepted the gift and denounced the giver to the Counter Intelligence Corps.

We decided to get away from Capri politics and do a little shopping before the Italians found out they were cobelligerents and raised the prices to their new co-allies. Chris invested a few hundred lire in souvenirs on the theory that the war might be over soon, and it would be good if the girls in Chicago remembered him. I had to find something which went well with pink. We found a little dress shop with a lovely black-haired girl behind the counter. Her English was nonexistent, but she had everything else and was eager to help. I made signs with my hands to show her the few small differences between Pinky's figure and her own.

Describing Pinky's color was a bit more difficult. But a piece of pale coral and a freckled Italian child solved that problem. Our girl flashed white teeth and began to pile silk stockings, underwear made of Florentine lace, colored skirts, and all kinds of things which girls can use but which I had never thought of.

Chris, who remained neutral in a corner, kept throwing pitying glances at me and different ones at the girl. The shop and my pocket were finally exhausted. While she was wrapping the stuff, I invited her to dinner. She picked up the piece of pink coral, put it in my hand, pointed to herself, and shook her head. Chris, who understood no Italian, but everything else, moved in. He took the coral from my hand and said: "Me, no, no, no" to the pink stone, and "Me, yes, yes, yes" to the girl. She did not speak enough English to argue with him.

—

Naples was no good. Rome would be better.

Between Naples and Rome Mr. Winston Churchill's "soft underbelly of Europe" was pregnant with hard mountains and well-placed German machine guns. The valleys between the mountains were soon filled with hospitals and cemeteries.

The rains started. The mud got deeper and deeper. Our shoes, designed for walking in garrison towns, thirstily drank in the water, and we slid two steps backward for each step forward. Our light shirts and trousers gave us no protection against the wind and rain. Our Army, the best equipped in the world, was stuck in those mountains, and it seemed we were not moving at all. With every costly five-hundred-yard advance, Rome seemed farther and farther away.

The newspapermen were not allowed, nor yet willing, to write the whole truth about the campaign. Besides, this was a job that pictures could do better than words. Here Bill Mauldin gave birth to his Willie and Joe, those two survivors of the fighting dogfaces of Italy. Here was the time for me to use my camera and like it. I dragged myself from mountain to mountain, from foxhole to foxhole, taking pictures of mud, misery, and death.

NEAR MOUNT PANTANO, NORTHEAST OF CASSINO, DECEMBER 1943.
*A soldier of the 2d Moroccan Infantry Division, which was composed
mostly of Berber soldiers and French officers. This division worked
closely with American forces.*

VENAFRO (NEAR CASSINO), DECEMBER 1943.
The rear command post of the U.S. 45th Infantry Division.

NEAR CASSINO, DECEMBER 1943–JANUARY 1944.

Opposite: NEAR CASSINO, JANUARY 1944. *An American soldier, foreground, carries a child to a safe refuge.*

In December I was climbing up the steep slopes of Mount Pantano. The 34th Infantry Division had been trying to reach the peak for the past ten or fifteen days, and had finally taken it the day before I arrived. The dead on the slopes were not yet buried.

Every five yards a foxhole, in each at least one dead soldier. Around them, torn covers of pocket books soaked through and through, empty cans of C-rations, and faded bits of letters from home. The bodies of those who had dared to leave their holes were blocking my path. Their blood was dry and rusty, blending with the color of the late autumn leaves fallen about them.

The higher I climbed, the shorter the distances between the dead. I could not look anymore. I stumbled on toward the hilltop, repeating to myself like an idiot, "I want to walk in the California sunshine and wear white shoes and white trousers." The correspondent's war neurosis was setting in.

From November to Christmas the Fifth Army advanced less than ten miles, sank ten inches deeper into the mud. My underwear was stiff under the uniform I never took off. My pictures were sad and empty as the war, and I didn't feel like sending them to the magazine.

Two days before Christmas I decided that the Fifth Army and I— we had had it. I knew that the war would not be decided in Italy. The latrine rumors had it that Eisenhower's headquarters would be moved back to London, and that Churchill couldn't delay the opening of the Second Front very much longer.

I decided to go back to Naples, change my underwear, and follow the war to London. I left the mountains and checked in at the headquarters of the 45th Division. I said good-bye, and asked for a jeep to take me to Naples.

———

Division headquarters consisted of a series of holes in the mud covered with tents. The G-2 tent was exceptionally busy. The staff was watching two sergeants paint little blue and red squares on an operations map. I wasn't interested, all I wanted was a jeep. A colonel pushed me over to the map, and explained how the attack would outflank Cassino and open the road to Rome. I said it was very interesting, and asked for the jeep. The colonel acted hurt, and said I would be sorry for leaving. I answered that I was sad as well as sorry, not to mention incredibly dirty and very tired.

The colonel got my point. He called over a captain, who looked at me and sniffed at me, and took me to his pup tent. There he opened a barracks bag full of priceless possessions. He fished out a set of fresh underwear, a clean uniform, a pair of shoes, and a bottle of Scotch. An orderly came in and brought three helmets full of hot water. I was washed, shaved, and dressed, and then they cleaned away my last objections with the whisky. The 45th Division must have been awfully keen to get their pictures in *Life* magazine.

That same night I was delivered to the advance headquarters of the 180th Infantry Regiment, and at four in the morning we jumped off.

The beginning of a night attack is not spectacular. One by one the soldiers pick up their equipment and start out at the slowest possible pace. In the darkness you can't see anything. You can hear only the noise made by the boots of the guy ahead of you. After every step your boots grow heavier, and fear squeezes your stomach into a small ball. The sweat on your face mixes with the early morning dew, and you remember every warm and comfortable room in which you have ever been.

By daylight you are ready to welcome any safe place, no matter how uncomfortable, and you have an irresistible desire to sit down behind the protection of the first big rock and smoke a cigarette. But you are not a coward, and you bypass the rock, knowing you will be sorry later on.

The first ray of sun announces the official zero hour, and our artillery promptly begins to soften up our objective. The outgoing shells are a great comfort, and they may even do some harm to the Germans. Unfortunately, they also wake them up. The German lieutenant on the hilltop picks up his glasses and his field telephone. A battery of German artillery places a shell in the middle of our column. The battery, according to the information of our G-2, is not supposed to be in our sector at all.

Everyone hits the mud and stops dreaming about home, stops speculating about the "if's" of our not being here, and the Germans maybe not being there. The hilltop is still two thousand yards away, and it is just as dangerous to stay as to go forward. So at every shell we hit the dirt, and then stand up and crouch forward until we hit the dirt again. Then someone yells for the first-aid men, and we are all sure that we will get it next.

We reach the last crest and there is our hilltop—only five hundred yards away. Our artillery is laying them in, and no German has any right to be still alive on that battered peak. We stand up to make a last rush for it, and the supposedly dead krauts open up with chattering machine guns and mortar fire.

Now we hit the dirt real hard; we don't intend to stand up again for a long time. Our platoon leader is calling battalion headquarters for more artillery and reinforcements. Meanwhile, the German mortars are systematically working over every square yard of the slope.

I am on my stomach, my head behind a big stone, my flanks protected by two soldiers lying next to me. After every explosion I raise my head, and I take a picture of the flattened soldiers ahead of me, and of the thin, drifting smoke of the explosion. Overhead, the pattern of shells is approaching my hole, and I don't raise my head anymore. A shell explodes ten yards away and something hits my behind. I am too scared to turn and look, the next one may hit even closer. Carefully, I feel my behind with my hand and find no blood, only a big rock which the exploding shell has thrown on me. The sergeant on my right gets a shrapnel which cuts his right arm just badly enough for a Purple Heart. The fellow on my left doesn't move at all, and will never get to open his Christmas package. Now the shells are falling way beyond us, and I light two cigarettes. The sergeant inhales deeply and hands me the first-aid packet. I fix his arm. Looking at the wound, he says, "By New Year's I'll be back in the lines."

Late in the afternoon the fire subsides, and the sergeant and I stand up and make a run for it. I have a dozen not unusual pictures, a big bruise on my behind, and my knees are wobbly. The Germans are still on the hilltop. I know it will be a long time before I want to go with any attack to take pictures again.

—

Naples hadn't changed much. Three months after our entry, the town was filled with dapper MP's in white helmets; "off limits" signs were posted everywhere; and the water was running again. The *Napolitanos* were doing a brisk business trading in the stuff they had stolen from our Army, while offering the *Americanos* everything from their wristwatches to their daughters. The ladies of active leisure walked up and down the Via Roma, with DDT powder in their hair. And Vesuvius, putting on its biggest show in a hundred years, poured forth soot and smoke that covered the entire city.

Bill Lang, who was now in charge of the *Time* and *Life* bureau, had miraculously succeeded in renting a hilltop apartment, complete with bathroom and running hot water—and I spent the entire first day after my arrival soaking in the tub. Next I shipped all my negatives to the magazine, under the title "This Is a Tough War," and asked my boss to transfer me to London, to cover the invasion of France. Two weeks later *Life* cabled that my "Tough War" story was just the thing, and would run in the magazine as a seven-page lead. Also, it was all right to go to London.

I put in a request for Army orders and began to pack. Bill Lang too was packing, over in his own corner. As I was holding Pinky's lace negligee, he was packing his long winter underwear and a pair of new combat boots. When I mentioned that I had cabled Pinky asking her to rent us the most elegant apartment in London, he didn't say a word, only showed me a new type of shovel for digging better foxholes. I hesitated; then I dropped Pinky's underflimsies and asked him what was cooking.

He led me to the window. The harbor of Naples was full of the same familiar invasion barges. For a war correspondent to miss an invasion is like refusing a date with Lana Turner after completing a five-year stretch in Sing Sing. I preferred Pinky to Turner—and five months at the front sure stretches your feelings, but I asked, "Can I still get in on the show?"

My innocent friend had it all fixed. "You're scheduled to go in with the Rangers. Colonel Darby is expecting you with your gear tomorrow morning."

I couldn't figure out where or how we were going to invade anything. The Fifth Army had in reserve only two war-weary divisions and a small battalion of Rangers. But at that time we still believed that the "powers-that-be" knew what they were doing, and we supposed that there were well-concealed armies loaded aboard boats, in the various ports of North Africa, all ready to join us. In this, our war, there were as yet no questions on general strategy. There were too few of us to ask any questions, no one to answer them.

I knew how long—and dry—waiting on an invasion boat can be, so I arrived at Colonel Darby's headquarters with a case of Spanish brandy. The colonel still didn't love photographers, but he seemed not to mind me—and thought the brandy might come in handy.

The Rangers had spent the last three weeks in a little harbor just north of Naples, waiting and preparing for the invasion, and many of them couldn't resist the advances of the ration-hungry Italian girls. It was a great time for fraternization; and the colonel wasn't against it. "A man who can't love, can't fight."

To mislead enemy spies and chattering women, the boys were ordered to spread the rumor that they were going home. The morning we embarked, hundreds of Italian crumpets came to say good-bye, to remind their friends not to forget to send them the visas, and to collect the remaining C-rations. It was a grotesque scene: the soldiers sitting on the docks, having their shoes shined; holding in their left hand a box of rations; in their right, the waist of their sweethearts.

By noon everyone was on the boats and we lifted anchor. Darby called me to the planning room and told me we were going to land on the Anzio beach, only fifty miles from Naples, at midnight. This was bad: I had expected a long boat trip and my case of brandy had cost $150 in the black market. We couldn't very well finish it in only twelve hours, and I couldn't see myself landing in water up to my neck carrying a case of brandy on my head.

Opposite: MOSCOSO NOTCH (NEAR CASSINO), JANUARY 4, 1944.
Fleeing the fighting in the mountains.

Bill Lang and I went back to our cabin, and asked the steward for a corkscrew. The steward, a friendly Cockney, looked at our brandy. Then he reminded us that this was a Royal Navy boat, and that the Royal Navy wasn't dry; in fact, we could buy as many bottles of Scotch as we pleased, at eight shillings a bottle. This was adding injury to injury. We ordered a bottle of Scotch, packed two bottles of brandy each in our bags, and distributed the remainder among the troops on board.

At midnight we were lowered onto the water in assault barges, and the British Navy delivered us without trouble into the waist-deep water forty yards from the beach.

We found no opposition while in the water, and the shooting on shore quieted down after about twenty minutes. The invasion was a total surprise, and we caught the Germans with most of their pants down. We put up headquarters in the basement of the luxurious casino, and I opened my bag so that I could take down my own wet pants.

The Spanish brandy, which had caused so much mental anguish during the day, had avenged itself for being neglected, quitting its bottles and spilling all over my change of clothes. I exchanged salt-water pants for brandy pants. I had an excellent "bouquet," it is true, but I was very uncomfortable during the night. In the morning the sun dried my pants, and my spirits revived. All the Germans were either dead or prisoners; and we found Italian salami, Swiss cheese, Norwegian sardines, Danish butter, and Münchner beer in their warehouses. The first twenty-four hours at Anzio were promising ones. Rome was only twenty-five miles away, and we expected to be there in less than two weeks. But those twenty-four hours were the only happy ones that anyone got to spend on that goddamned beach.

The Public Relations Office had requisitioned a villa on the beach, and I found the correspondents all safe and happy there. While waiting for news from corps headquarters, we started a poker game. Outside, we could see the steady stream of boats arriving in the harbor, unloading men and guns. Between games I got up and took pictures from the window. Anzio was still the most pleasant of assignments.

In the middle of a draw-poker game, our antiaircraft guns opened fire. I rushed to the window. Twenty-four German bombers were flying in the blue sky just above our villa. They dropped their eggs on the unloading ships. I focused my camera and got a beautiful shot of a freighter blowing up, not two hundred yards away.

The bombers left, and I returned to the game, saying what a terrific picture I had just taken. Clark Lee was impatiently fingering his cards. "Can't you keep shoptalk out of a poker game?"

I looked at my hand and saw that I had a pair of fives. That isn't much power in a draw game, but I resented Clark's attitude toward my profession. I raised a hundred dollars, hoping for no call.

Don Whitehead, of the AP, looked at his cards, then at my face. "You Hungarian fake," he said. "You don't have a damn thing in your hand. I raise two hundred."

When Clark's turn came, he said, "I don't care for the trend, but I'm going to find out who's bluffing." He raised again, pushing all his money to the center of the table.

This looked like the poker game to end poker games. We called the raise, and then began to draw. Whitehead said he would stand pat, while Clark Lee asked for one card. I asked for three. It was obvious that my fives didn't stand a chance. We had already bet all our money, and we simply laid up our cards. Whitehead had a straight, but Clark Lee produced the flush he had drawn. Whitehead grunted, and Clark reached for the money.

I didn't particularly care to look at my cards, and turned them up one at a time. The first two were my pair of fives; the third was a lucky third five; the fourth, a three; and the decisive fifth, another five—four fives in all.

But it was the last time I was to win at poker for the rest of the war. In its own way, it was as much a mistake as that easy landing at Anzio.

———

The fifth day at Anzio, we knew we were not going to be in Rome for a long time, that we would be lucky to hold the small piece of land we had taken the very first day. The Germans outnumbered us, and there was not a square yard of the bridgehead that they couldn't observe or fill with shells.

The newspapermen moved down into the basement of the press villa, and we thought twice before we ventured out. Every time I sat in my jeep, I put my bedroll between my legs. I figured that if I got hit now, just before my London vacation, they had better shoot my head off.

My orders for London were still in my pocket, and every day I decided to leave on the morrow.

There were no new pictures to take on that accursed bridgehead, where every morning we learned that during the night one of our best men had gone. We did not gamble, we did not drink, we did not shave. We did not file any stories, and, like the soldiers, waited only for that shell or for the spring.

The end of February, I received a message from Chris. The 9th Troop Carrier Command was being transferred to London, and he had a plane waiting for me in Naples.

I left Anzio on a hospital ship—one man unhurt among that boatload of badly wounded.

VIII

We took off and circled once over Naples. From one thousand feet up, the town looked beautiful again, and the war began to recede into the distance. We flew over Salerno, and could see the masts of sunken ships sticking out of the water. From the air, the new ruins of Sicilian towns did not look very different from the two-thousand-year-old ruins of Agrigento.

The places that made front-page headlines only six months before were simple pastures now, thickly planted with shell holes. Retracing the road our Army had traveled was like visiting a movie set two weeks after the picture is finished—some of the props were still lying around. As for the sea, it is the most secretive of sets. There, the props lie silently under the water.

We left the North African coast behind. We put aside our past three campaigns and would not talk of the one to come. Chris and I talked about what we were going to do during our first twenty-four hours in London. I counted on arriving just before noon. I would su[r]prise Pinky in the magnificent establishment she had rented for [   ] There, while I sat in the bathtub, she would prepare a breakf[ast of] fresh eggs, jam, toast. Later, I would put on a dark blue suit a[nd   ] shirt, and she would put her hair up and wear her best eve[ning   ]

Dinner at Boulestin's, and a bottle of Krug, 1928. Then we would go over to the Cocoanut Grove, and Chris could join us there and would be allowed two dances with Pinky.

Chris listened to this schedule and said that Pinky must undoubtedly have a girlfriend. I assured him that Pinky had dozens of girlfriends and he would have no trouble at all.

We arrived in London at seven in the evening. The building where Pinky had rented us an apartment was the grandest house on Belgrave Square. The names of the occupants were stuck in white letters on a large black bulletin board in the lobby. The first floor was occupied by the dowager of something; Lord so-and-so and Air Marshal X took up the second and third; the fascist Spanish ambassador had the fourth floor, a doctor the fifth, and a lieutenant commander the sixth. Above all of that were Capa and Pinky in the penthouse.

Chris and I took the elevator up to the top floor. I put my key in the lock and buzzed three times as I opened the door. The hall inside was empty, but there was a light on and a sound of activity was coming from one of the rooms. A stomach followed by a girl appeared in the doorway. She was young, her face pretty under light brown hair, and her child was probably overdue.

Chris was embarrassed. "Why didn't you say so?" he asked me.

The girl looked us both over and turned to me. "You must be Capa. I'm Mona Kline, a friend of Elaine's."

"Didn't I tell you," I said to Chris, "that Pinky would have a friend?" I told Mona I was glad to meet her. "Where is Pinky?" I wanted to know.

She hesitated. "Her appendix beat you to it," she said, then quickly added, as she saw my face, "but she's perfectly all right now." She explained that Pinky had been expecting me for the past four weeks and that she had put off the operation from day to day. Last night, however, her appendix had burst, and she had been rushed off to the hospital. "She's already been allowed to talk to me over the phone," she assured me. "But I think you had better wait until morning. She shouldn't get too excited."

I spent that evening with Chris in the nearest pub. During the night, while I lay with my eyes open, he snored happily at my side in our enormous Louis XIV bed.

Early in the morning, I went out and bought all kinds of flowers. Arms laden, I worked my way into the hospital. A little nurse greeted me at Pinky's door. "I'm so glad you've arrived, Mr. Parker. Your wife was crying for you all through the anesthetic."

A pale, pink spot on a white pillow whispered, "Please turn away, my Capa." I turned and faced the wall until she said, "Now."

The pink spot now had eyes, eyelashes, and lips, and the room smelled of Arpège. Her mascara was already running. "I tried so hard to wait for you...." The eyes dried up quickly and the real Pinky spoke. "The scar on my tummy will be like the Croix de Lorraine—very pretty, and soon very faint."

I found my voice. I promised her I would cherish the improvement. The doctor came in and shook hands with me. He addressed me as Mr. Parker. I asked him to call me by my nickname, Capa. He took me out in the corridor and told me we would have to be very careful, that she had waited too long with the operation. I felt very sick.

After the doctor left, a kind lady entered and came over to me. "I am Elaine's mother, and you are a very bad boy." We were allowed to stay a little while longer, and we all had a pleasant family conversation.

———

In May 1944, London had invasion fever. The town was jammed with uniforms of the United Nations, and whisky was scarce in the pubs. The only oasis in that desert was a place called The Little French Club. It had been founded by an intellectual English lady with French sympathies. The Free French were the least paid and also the thirstiest of the United Nations forces, and The Little French Club charged a minimum for drinks. In addition, it had a miraculous supply of Scotch. Irwin Shaw and Bill Saroyan, both suffering intellectuals with the rank of private in the American Army, convinced the lady that they had great admiration for the French, and they were accepted into the coterie. The news of their beachhead on Free French territory soon spread to other thirsty intellectuals, and the infiltration began. In my quest for sympathy and Scotch, I was advised to try and qualify for the club. The quota for the American membership was more than filled, but I managed anyway. I was accepted as a Free Hungarian.

That was where I spent the second evening of my London holiday. At 3:00 A.M. I found my way to my Belgravian splendor. My house guest, Mona, was up. She was so much up that it took me no time at all to figure out that I could be expecting a second house guest any minute. I rushed her to the maternity hospital. Mona was so highly qualified that she was accepted without hesitation, and I was sent down to the prospective fathers' department. An expectant father in an American uniform was still a rare sight in London, and the worried English fathers forgot about themselves for the moment and swarmed all over me, assuring me that everything would be all right.

At eleven, a nurse came in and announced: "Mr. Kline, you're the father of a beautiful baby boy."

———

Chris came back on a twenty-four-hour leave from the Midlands, where the 9th Troop Carrier Command was stationed. He admired Mr. Kline's little boy, and then we went over to Pinky's hospital, where he admired Mr. Parker's pink girl. In the evening I took him over to The Little French Club, where he had great success as a storyteller. He told the story of Mr. Parker and Mr. Kline, which made me out to be the poor man's Dr. Jekyll and Mr. Hyde—played by Abbott and Costello. The American expatriates showed their appreciation of the story the following day by filling Mona's and Pinky's rooms full of flowers, PX rations—and visitors.

———

The invasion rumors and the arrivals of Very Important People increased daily. Ernest Hemingway, hidden behind a tremendous brown-gray beard, was one of the last to join the members of The Little French Club. He was a sore sight for sore eyes, but I was really happy to see him again. Our friendship dated from the good days. We first met in 1937 in Loyalist Spain, where I was a young freelance photographer, and he was a very famous writer. His nickname was "Papa" anyway, and I soon adopted him as a father. In the years between, he had many occasions to fulfill his parental obligations, and now was glad to see his adopted son in no obvious need for cash. To prove my devotion and prosperity, I decided to give him a party in my useless and very expensive apartment.

On my daily visit to the hospital, I told Pinky about my idea, and she approved on condition that I smuggle her a split of champagne for the occasion. She revealed that hidden away in her clothes closet were ten bottles of Scotch and eight bottles of gin which she had saved from her liquor ration during the ten months I was gone.

Scotch and gin were very civilly rationed, but brandy and champagne were very easy to buy for thirty dollars a bottle. On the day of the great event, I bought a fish bowl, a case of champagne, some brandy, and a half-dozen fresh peaches. I soaked the peaches in the brandy, poured the champagne over them, and everything was ready.

The attraction of free booze combined with Mr. Hemingway proved irresistible. Everyone was in London for the invasion, and they all showed up at the party. They drank the Scotch, they drank the champagne, and the brandy and gin too.

My guest of honor sat in a corner talking to a doctor friend of mine about the benevolent cancer, or barber's itch, that had obliged him to grow the beard.

At four in the morning, we reached the peaches. The bottles were empty, the fish bowl dry, and the guests began to trickle away. The doctor offered to give Hemingway a lift to his hotel. I ate the peaches and went to sleep.

At 7:00 A.M. my telephone rang. The hospital was calling. They said something about a Mr. Hemingway and asked me to come down to the emergency room. There, on an operating table, I found 215 pounds of Papa. His skull was split wide open and his beard was full of blood. The doctors were about to give him an anesthetic and sew his head together. Papa politely thanked me for the party. He asked me to look after the doctor, who had driven him into a water tank, and who must have been hurt pretty badly too. Also, I was to notify

LONDON, MAY 1944. *Ernest Hemingway recovers in the hospital following a party given by Capa. Hemingway was injured when the car in which he was riding home, through the city's blacked-out streets, crashed into a steel water tank.*

his children in the States that whatever they might read in the papers, he was not badly hurt. After forty-eight little stitches, Papa's head looked better than new.

In the emergency room, where they heard me calling him "Papa," I became known as Mr. Capa Hemingway.

———

It was the end of May. The sun was hot in England, the invasion long overdue, and the hospitals not funny anymore. I loved Pinky, but I wanted to go back to war now and return when she could wait for me at the station. I hated to go to the hospital, and I hated to be kicking around in the same town where she was imprisoned by flowers and nurses. Pinky hated it worse than I.

Finally, she was released from the hospital on the condition that she spend at least two weeks in a nursing home. The nursing home was at Ascot, thirty miles from London, and was run by the Sisters of the Order of St. Mary.

I carried Pinky to the hired car. I told the driver to take the road to Ascot. "26 Belgrave Square," said Pinky. I repeated, "The road to Ascot, please." Pinky said, "You have no right…it is my tummy." It was her tummy but it was not hers to choose.

Leaving the outskirts of London, the fields were green and we ran into spring. "It will be for only two weeks," I said.

"I'll never forgive you a day of it."

The Sisters were kind, her room was comfortable, and the view from her window lovely. But I had to go back to London.

The Little French Club was a bore, Belgravia a horror, and I was not happy at all. On my last visit to the nursing home, I found Pinky walking in the garden. Her skirt fit her waist again. Her legs were pretty to look at, if a bit wobbly to walk on. She was due home the day after next. We walked back to her room and a Sister served us tea. We drank the tea, and I told her that a bottle of the best champagne was cooling in our icebox. The Sister came back to take away the tray, and told me that visiting time was over. I was in uniform, and the newspaper on Pinky's table read: INVASION ON SUNDAY SAYS HITLER. The Sister picked up the tray and walked toward the door. Without turning, she said: "If you leave after darkness, no one will notice you."

———

Out of hundreds of war correspondents, only a few dozen were chosen to accompany the first of the invasion forces. Among them were four photographers, and I was one.

The Public Relations Office held a meeting for the chosen few and told us that from now on our equipment must always be packed, and we weren't to wander from our apartments for more than an hour at a time.

There was no way I could get out to Ascot.

I had everything I needed, but decided to do a little invasion shopping anyway. I bought an English Army raincoat at Burberrys, and a silver pocket flask at Dunhill's. I was ready.

Very early on the day that Pinky was due back, a lieutenant from the Public Relations Office woke me up and said he would help me carry my equipment. I wasn't permitted to talk to anyone or leave any messages. But the rent was due, and he let me sign my name on a blank check and leave it on the dressing table under a bottle of Arpège. I felt that Pinky would understand.

IX

Once a year, usually sometime in April, every self-respecting Jewish family celebrates Passover, the Jewish Thanksgiving. The Passover celebration proceeds along the well-known lines of Thanksgiving, the only difference between the two being that the Passover feast has everything and turkey too, and that the children of the very old world get even more sick than those of the very new world.

When dinner is irrevocably over, father loosens his belt and lights a five-cent cigar. At this crucial moment the youngest of the sons— I have been doing it for years—steps up and addresses his father in solemn Hebrew. He asks, "What makes this day different from all other days?" Then father, with great relish and gusto, tells the story of how, many thousands of years ago in Egypt, the angel of destruction passed over the firstborn sons of the Chosen People, and how, afterwards, General Moses led them across the Red Sea without getting their feet wet.

The Gentiles and Jews who crossed the English Channel on the sixth of June in the year 1944, landing with very wet feet on the beach in Normandy called "Easy Red," ought to have—once a year, on that date—a Crossover day. Their children, after finishing a couple of cans of C-rations, would ask their father, "What makes this day different from all other days?" The story that I would tell might sound like this:

The men who were condemned to spend that spring on the French beaches were gathered in immense concentration camps on the southeast coast of England. The camps were surrounded by barbed wire, and once you entered the gates you were halfway across the Channel.

Inside, we were being processed for our trip. We had to exchange our legitimate dollar bills and pound notes for invasion francs printed on flimsy paper. We received a list containing hundreds of items which told what the well-dressed visitor would be wearing on the French beaches during the 1944 season. In addition, we received a little book telling us how to treat and address the natives there. There were some useful approaches in French. *"Bonjour, monsieur, nous sommes les amis américains."* That was for addressing the men. *"Bonjour, mademoiselle, voulez-vous faire une promenade avec moi?"* That was for the girls. The first one meant "Mister, don't shoot me," and the other could mean anything.

There were still other suggestions dealing with the natives of a different country, whom we expected—for certain reasons—to meet in numbers on those beaches. These consisted of convenient German phrases which promised cigarettes, hot baths, and all sorts of comforts, all in exchange for the simple act of unconditional surrender. Indeed, the booklet made promising reading.

Every piece of our clothing had to be gasproofed, waterproofed, and camouflaged in the many various colors of our future landscape. Thus prepared, we were ready and waiting for the day called "D."

We were all suffering from that strange sickness known as "amphibia." Being amphibious troops had only one meaning for us: we would have to be unhappy in the water before we could be unhappy on the shore. There were no exceptions. The only character who is amphibious and happy at the same time is the alligator. There were different degrees of "amphibia" and those who were scheduled to be the first to reach the beach had it the worst.

ON BOARD THE U.S. COAST GUARD TRANSPORT SHIP *SAMUEL CHASE*, AT ANCHOR OFF WEYMOUTH, ENGLAND, JUNE 1–5, 1944. *Planning the details of the D-Day landings, using a model of the section of the Normandy coast that had been code-named Omaha Beach.*

The harbor of Weymouth was having a grand time. Battleships, troopships, freighters, and invasion barges all mingled together. Floating in the air above them was a balloon barrage made up of many hundreds of silver blimps. The prospective tourists to France were sunbathing on the decks of the boats and lazily watching the giant toys that were being hoisted aboard. For the optimists, everything looked like a new secret weapon, especially from a distance.

On my boat, the U.S.S. *Chase,* the population fell into three categories: the planners, the gamblers, and the writers of last letters. The gamblers were to be found on the upper deck, clustering around a pair of tiny dice and putting thousands of dollars on the blanket. The last-letter-writers hid in corners and were putting down beautiful sentences on paper leaving their favorite shotguns to kid brothers and their dough to the family. As for the planners, they were down in the gymnasium in the bottom of the ship, lying on their stomachs around a rubber carpet on which was placed a miniature of every house and tree on the French coast. The platoon leaders picked their way between the rubber villages and looked for protection behind the rubber trees and in the rubber ditches on the mattress.

We also had a tiny model of every ship, and low on the walls were signs giving the names of the beaches and the specific sectors: "Fox Green," "Easy Red," and others, all parts of the "Omaha" beach. The naval commander and his staff had joined the gymnasium and they were pushing the little ships around in order to reach the beaches that were painted on the walls. They pushed them around very expertly. In fact, the more I looked at these bemedaled gents playing on the floor, the more I was filled with terrific confidence.

I followed the proceedings on the gymnasium floor with more than polite interest. The U.S.S. *Chase* was a mother ship which carried many assault barges which it would release ten miles off the French coast. I would have to make up my mind and choose a barge to ride in and a rubber tree to hide behind on the shore. It was like watching a lot of race horses ten minutes before starting time. In five minutes the bets would have to be placed.

On the one hand, the objectives of Company B looked interesting, and to go along with them seemed to be a pretty safe bet. Then again, I used to know Company E very well and the story I had got with them in Sicily was one of my best during the war. I was about to choose between Companies B and E when Colonel Taylor, commander of the 16th Infantry Regiment of the 1st Division, the attacking force, tipped me off that regimental headquarters would follow close behind the first waves of infantry. If I went with him, I wouldn't miss the action, and I'd be a little safer. This sounded like the real favorite—an even-money bet—two to one to be alive in the evening.

If at this point my son should interrupt me, and ask, "What is the difference between the war correspondent and any other man in uniform?" I would say that the war correspondent gets more drinks, more girls, better pay, and greater freedom than the soldier, but that at this stage of the game, having the freedom to choose his spot and being allowed to be a coward and not be executed for it is his torture. The war correspondent has his stake—his life—in his own hands, and he can put it on this horse or that horse, or he can put it back in his pocket at the very last minute.

I am a gambler. I decided to go in with Company E in the first wave.

Once I decided to go in with the first assault troops I began to convince myself that the invasion would be a pushover and that all this talk about an "impregnable west wall" was just German propaganda. I went up on deck and took a good look at the disappearing English coast. The pale green glow of the vanishing island hit my soft spot and I joined the legion of the last-letter-writers. My brother could have my ski boots and my mother could invite someone from England to stay with her. The idea was disgusting, and I never mailed the letter. I folded it up, and stuck it in my breast pocket.

Now I joined the third category. At 2:00 A.M. the ship's loudspeaker broke up our poker game. We placed our money in waterproof money belts and were brutally reminded that the Thing was imminent.

They fixed a gas mask, an inflatable lifebelt, a shovel, and some other gadgets around me, and I placed my very expensive Burberry raincoat over my arm. I was the most elegant invader of them all.

AT ANCHOR OFF OMAHA BEACH, NORMANDY, JUNE 6, 1944.
*Early on the morning of D-Day, American troops board the
transports that will carry them to the beachhead.*

—

Our preinvasion breakfast was served at 3:00 A.M. The mess boys of the U.S.S. *Chase* wore immaculate white jackets and served hot cakes, sausages, eggs, and coffee with unusual zest and politeness. But the preinvasion stomachs were preoccupied, and most of the noble effort was left on the plates.

At 4:00 A.M. we were assembled on the open deck. The invasion barges were swinging on the cranes, ready to be lowered. Waiting for the first ray of light, the two thousand men stood in perfect silence; whatever they were thinking, it was some kind of prayer.

I too stood very quietly. I was thinking a little bit of everything: of green fields, pink clouds, grazing sheep, all the good times, and very much of getting the best pictures of the day. None of us was at all impatient, and we wouldn't have minded standing in the darkness for a very long time. But the sun had no way of knowing that this day was different from all others, and rose on its usual schedule. The first-wavers stumbled into their barges, and—as if on slow-moving elevators—we descended onto the sea. The sea was rough and we were wet before our barge pushed away from the mother ship. It was already clear that General Eisenhower would not lead his people across the Channel with dry feet or dry else.

In no time, the men started to puke. But this was a polite as well as a carefully prepared invasion, and little paper bags had been provided for the purpose. Soon the puking hit a new low. I had an idea this would develop into the father and mother of all D-Days.

The coast of Normandy was still miles away when the first unmistakable popping reached our listening ears. We ducked down in the puky water in the bottom of the barge and ceased to watch the approaching coastline. The first empty barge, which had already unloaded its troops on the beach, passed us on the way back to the *Chase*, and the Negro boatswain gave us a happy grin and the V sign. It was now light enough to start taking pictures, and I brought my first Contax camera out of its waterproof oilskin. The flat bottom of our barge hit the earth of France. The boatswain lowered the steel-covered barge front, and there, between the grotesque designs of steel obstacles sticking out of the water, was a thin line of land covered with smoke—our Europe, the "Easy Red" beach.

My beautiful France looked sordid and uninviting, and a German machine gun, spitting bullets around the barge, fully spoiled my return. The men from my barge waded in the water. Waist-deep, with rifles ready to shoot, with the invasion obstacles and the smoking beach in the background—this was good enough for the photographer. I paused for a moment on the gangplank to take my first real picture of the invasion. The boatswain, who was in an understandable hurry to get the hell out of there, mistook my picture-taking attitude for explicable hesitation, and helped me make up my mind with a well-aimed kick in the rear. The water was cold, and the beach still more than a hundred yards away. The bullets tore holes in the water around me, and I made for the nearest steel obstacle. A soldier got there at the same time, and for a few minutes we shared its cover. He took the waterproofing off his rifle and began to shoot without much aiming at the smoke-hidden beach. The sound of his rifle gave him enough courage to move forward and he left the obstacle to me. It was a foot larger now, and I felt safe enough to take pictures of the other guys hiding just like I was.

It was still very early and very gray for good pictures, but the gray water and the gray sky made the little men, dodging under the surrealistic designs of Hitler's anti-invasion brain trust, very effective.

I finished my pictures, and the sea was cold in my trousers. Reluctantly, I tried to move away from my steel pole, but the bullets chased me back every time. Fifty yards ahead of me, one of our half-burnt amphibious tanks stuck out of the water and offered me my next cover. I sized up the situation. There was little future for the elegant raincoat heavy on my arm. I dropped it and made for the tank. Between floating bodies I reached it, paused for a few more pictures, and gathered my guts for the last jump to the beach.

Now the Germans played on all their instruments, and I could not find any hole between the shells and bullets that blocked the last twenty-five yards to the beach. I just stayed behind my tank, repeating a little sentence from my Spanish Civil War days, "*Es una cosa muy seria. Es una cosa muy seria.*" This is a very serious business.

The tide was coming in and now the water reached the farewell letter to my family in my breast pocket. Behind the human cover of the last two guys, I reached the beach. I threw myself flat and my lips touched the earth of France. I had no desire to kiss it.

Jerry still had plenty of ammunition left, and I fervently wished I could be beneath the earth now and above later. The chances to the contrary were becoming increasingly strong. I turned my head sideways and found myself nose to nose with a lieutenant from our last night's poker game. He asked me if I knew what he saw. I told him no and that I didn't think he could see much beyond my head. "I'll tell you what I see," he whispered. "I see my ma on the front porch, waving my insurance policy."

———

St. Laurent-sur-Mer must have been at one time a drab, cheap resort for vacationing French schoolteachers. Now, on June 6, 1944, it was the ugliest beach in the whole world. Exhausted from the water and the fear, we lay flat on a small strip of wet sand between the sea and the barbed wire. The slant of the beach gave us some protection, so long as we lay flat, from the machine-gun and rifle bullets, but the tide pushed us against the barbed wire, where the guns were enjoying open season. I crawled on my stomach over to my friend Larry, the Irish padre of the regiment, who could swear better than any amateur. He growled at me, "You damn half-Frenchy! If you didn't like it here, why the hell did you come back?" Thus comforted by religion, I took out my second Contax camera and began to shoot without raising my head.

From the air, "Easy Red" must have looked like an open tin of sardines. Shooting from the sardine's angle, the foreground of my pictures was filled with wet boots and green faces. Above the boots and faces, my picture frames were filled with shrapnel smoke; burnt tanks and sinking barges formed my background. Larry had a dry cigarette. I reached in my hip pocket for my silver flask and offered

Overleafs: OMAHA BEACH, NEAR COLLEVILLE-SUR-MER, NORMANDY COAST, JUNE 6, 1944. *The first wave of American troops lands on D-Day.*

OMAHA BEACH, JUNE 6, 1944.

OMAHA BEACH, JUNE 6, 1944.

it to Larry. He tilted his head sideways and took a swig from the corner of his mouth. Before returning the bottle, he gave it to my other chum, the Jewish medic, who very successfully imitated Larry's technique. The corner of my mouth was good enough for me too.

The next mortar shell fell between the barbed wire and the sea, and every piece of shrapnel found a man's body. The Irish priest and the Jewish doctor were the first to stand up on the "Easy Red" beach. I shot the picture. The next shell fell even closer. I didn't dare to take my eyes off the finder of my Contax and frantically shot frame after frame. Half a minute later, my camera jammed—my roll was finished. I reached in my bag for a new roll, and my wet, shaking hands ruined the roll before I could insert it in my camera.

I paused for a moment...and then I had it bad.

The empty camera trembled in my hands. It was a new kind of fear shaking my body from toe to hair, and twisting my face. I unhooked my shovel and tried to dig a hole. The shovel hit stone under the sand and I hurled it away. The men around me lay motionless. Only the dead on the waterline rolled with the waves. An LCI braved the fire and medics with red crosses painted on their helmets poured from it. I did not think and I didn't decide it. I just stood up and ran toward the boat. I stepped into the sea between two bodies and the water reached to my neck. The rip tide hit my body and every wave slapped my face under my helmet. I held my cameras high above my head, and suddenly I knew that I was running away. I tried to turn but couldn't face the beach, and told myself, "I am just going to dry my hands on that boat."

I reached the boat. The last medics were just getting out. I climbed aboard. As I reached the deck I felt a shock, and suddenly was all covered with feathers. I thought, "What is this? Is somebody killing chickens?" Then I saw that the superstructure had been shot away and that the feathers were the stuffing from the kapok jackets of the men that had been blown up. The skipper was crying. His assistant had been blown up all over him and he was a mess.

Our boat was listing and we slowly pulled away from the beach to try and reach the mother ship before we sank. I went down to the engine room, dried my hands, and put fresh films in both cameras. I got up on deck again in time to take one last picture of the smoke-covered beach. Then I took some shots of the crew giving transfusions on the open deck. An invasion barge came alongside and took us off the sinking boat. The transfer of the badly wounded on the heavy seas was a difficult business. I took no more pictures. I was busy lifting stretchers. The barge brought us to the U.S.S. *Chase,* the very boat I had left only six hours before. On the *Chase,* the last wave of the 16th Infantry was just being lowered, but the decks were already full with returning wounded and dead.

This was my last chance to return to the beach. I did not go. The mess boys who had served our coffee in white jackets and with white gloves at three in the morning were covered with blood and were sewing the dead in white sacks. The sailors were hoisting stretchers from sinking barges alongside. I started taking pictures. Then things got confused....

———

I woke up in a bunk. My naked body was covered with a rough blanket. On my neck, a piece of paper read: "Exhaustion case. No dog tags." My camera bag was on the table, and I remembered who I was.

In the second bunk was another naked young man, his eyes staring at the ceiling. The tag around his neck said only: "Exhaustion case." He said: "I am a coward." He was the only survivor from the ten amphibious tanks that had preceded the first waves of infantry. All these tanks had sunk in the heavy seas. He said he should have stayed back on the beach. I told him that I should have stayed on the beach myself.

The engines were humming; our boat was on its way back to England. During the night the man from the tank and I both beat our breasts, each insisting that the other was blameless, that the only coward was himself.

———

In the morning we docked at Weymouth. A score of hungry newspapermen who had not been allowed to go along on the invasion were waiting for us on the pier to get the first personal experience stories of the men who had reached the beachhead and returned. I learned that the only other war correspondent photographer as-

OFF OMAHA BEACH, JUNE 6, 1944.
Medical transport craft for men wounded in the first wave.

ON BOARD THE U.S.S. *HENRICO*, OFF OMAHA BEACH, JUNE 6, 1944.
The bodies of some of the men killed in the first wave.

signed to the "Omaha" beach had returned two hours earlier and had never left his boat, never touched the beach. He was now on his way back to London with his terrific scoop.

I was treated as a hero. I was offered a plane to take me to London to give a broadcast of my experience. But I still remembered the night enough, and refused. I put my films in the press bag, changed my clothes, and returned to the beachhead a few hours later on the first available boat.

Seven days later, I learned that the pictures I had taken on "Easy Red" were the best of the invasion. But the excited darkroom assistant, while drying the negatives, had turned on too much heat and the emulsions had melted and run down before the eyes of the London office. Out of one hundred and six pictures in all, only eight were salvaged. The captions under the heat-blurred pictures read that Capa's hands were badly shaking.

X

Back on the beach that night, I found my colleagues in the barn of a Norman farmhouse, where they had established the first press camp in France. They were squatting on the straw around a couple of half-burned candles, drinking a yellow liquid from a gallon keg. A closed typewriter served as a table.

The day was D-plus-two, the drink was a Norman applejack called Calvados, and the party was a French wake in my honor. I had been reported dead by a sergeant who had seen my body floating on the water with my cameras around my neck. I had been missing for forty-eight hours, my death had become official, and my obituaries had just been released by the censor. The sudden materialization of my thirsty ghost filled my friends with disgust at their wasted sentiment, and they introduced me to the Calvados.

———

Our bridgehead was far too small to supply 200,000 invaders with Calvados. The price of the awful stuff was four times doubled by the time we were ready to expand and begin our attack on Cherbourg. Cherbourg was an important harbor; besides, all the intelligence reports mentioned that the German fortress had a supply dump full of fine French liquors that had been requisitioned by the Wehrmacht. Unfortunately, the reports also mentioned a hell of a lot of guns of every caliber.

OMAHA BEACH, JUNE 1944. *French fishermen look at the bodies of some of the men killed during the D-Day landings. Barrage balloons, visible in the sky, are moored over the landing area to confuse enemy aircraft and to prevent them from flying in low.*

OMAHA BEACH, JUNE 1944. *The beachhead several days after D-Day.*

OMAHA BEACH, JUNE 1944.
A German soldier captured by American forces.

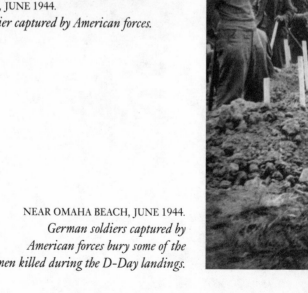

NEAR OMAHA BEACH, JUNE 1944.
*German soldiers captured by
American forces bury some of the
men killed during the D-Day landings.*

NORMANDY BEACHHEAD, JUNE 1944.
General Omar N. Bradley, who had recently had a boil on his nose lanced.

NORMANDY, JUNE 1944. *A German general surrenders to American officers.*

Overleaf: NORMANDY, JUNE–JULY 1944. *American soldiers.*

I joined the 9th Infantry Division for the attack. The 9th was one of our most experienced fighting groups, and its commander, Major General Eddy, was a pushing kind of soldier. The Germans were tough in their well-prepared fortress, but not so tough that they fought to the last German—only to the first American that got close enough to be dangerous. Then they threw up their hands, shouted *"Kamerad!"* and asked for cigarettes. The division took pillbox after pillbox. My nerve came back and I took a lot of pictures of close fighting.

The morning of our final attack on Cherbourg, I joined a battalion of the 47th Regiment. With me were Ernie Pyle and my dignified boss, Charles Wertenbaker, who was head of the *Time* and *Life* European staff. We felt that the 47th had the best chance of being first to reach the center of town. We were fed up with being shot at, but too thirsty to stay behind. It was pouring rain as we entered the first streets. The Germans were sniping at us from the windows, and we kept close to the walls and jumped from door to door for cover.

Charlie said he was too old to be playing Indian; Ernie said he was too old and too scared; I said I was too young and, besides, I couldn't take pictures in the rain.

We didn't give a damn about being the first correspondents in Cherbourg, but we wanted to get to that warehouse. So we kept right on, dragging on the tail of our battalion.

We reached the first objective: the Cherbourg military hospital. About two hundred fifty wounded prisoners from the 82d Airborne Division were liberated—also a considerable supply of the very best French bottles in the basement. Ernie went to talk to the prisoners, Charlie interviewed the German doctor, and I made for the cellar. I was late. Every soldier of the 47th Infantry already had his arms, jacket, and pockets bulging with precious bottles. I begged one of them for just a single bottle, but he laughed and said, "Only if you're Ernie Pyle." With the next soldier, my approach was different. I asked him for a bottle for Ernie Pyle, and he parted with it willingly. Soon I had collected my loot of Benedictine and brandy. Neither Charlie nor Ernie uttered a single word of protest.

NOTRE-DAME-DE-CENILLY, SOUTHWEST OF ST.-LÔ, JULY 28, 1944.
A French farmer offers cider to the men of an American armored unit.

SOUTHWEST OF ST.-LÔ, JULY 26–30, 1944.
Men of the U.S. 2d Armored Division under fire.

Meanwhile, General Eddy had got his own loot: General von Schlieben, the German commander of Cherbourg. He was our first high-ranking prisoner, and I wanted his picture badly. But he turned his back, refused to pose, and told his aide in German that he was bored with the whole idea of American press liberties. In German, I replied, "And I am bored with photographing defeated German generals." He became furious and turned sharply about at me. I snapped his picture. It couldn't have been better.

———

Breaking through at St.-Lô, our First Army opened up the German lines, and General Patton's heavily armored and motorized Third Army pulled through the breach. I joined Patton's fast-moving 4th Armored Division as it drove toward Brittany along the coastal road. On both sides of the road, the happy French were shouting *"Bonne Chance!"* And the happy signposts read: "90 kilometers...80 kilometers...to Paris."

The first towns through which we drove had suffered much from our heavy raids. Our tactical air force had bombed them to shambles in order to cut off the communications of the retreating Germans. In those towns, the French were only half happy and complained that if we had dropped as many arms to the French underground as bombs on the innocent French towns, we would have killed more Germans and fewer Frenchmen, and succeeded better in our objective.

The little coastal town of Bréhal was the first town we reached that was unscarred by war. The Germans were on the run, and the good campaign began. Here the French were full happy. The food was good, and the first glass of wine was free in the bars.

The French Resistance was strong and well represented in this little town. Young boys and girls with rifles on their shoulders came and placed themselves at our disposal. Their meeting place was the Petit Hotel, and there I made my personal headquarters for the night.

The *patron* of the hotel was a member of the Resistance himself. He said he had hidden and saved his very last bottle of the finest champagne for this very occasion. He invited over two young and shapely girls of the Resistance and we opened the bottle with a great

NORMANDY, JUNE–JULY 1944.

ALENÇON, NORMANDY, AUGUST 12, 1944. *Welcoming American troops.*

NEAR CHARTRES, AUGUST 1944.

NORMANDY, JUNE–JULY 1944. *An American chaplain attends to a dying German soldier.*

Opposite: NORMANDY, JUNE–JULY 1944. *An American military policeman searches a captured German SS officer.*

ceremony. A young major in the 1st Infantry Division, Paul Gael, who had no business whatever in this sector, turned up on a very personal tour of inspection. I knew him from before, and he joined the party. Our champagne was soon gone, but the *patron* remembered that he had one more last bottle. In fact, we drank many last bottles that evening. Gael taught jitterbug steps to the Resistance, while they taught him basic French.

At midnight, the *patron* grew sleepy and the girls slung their rifles on their backs, saying that they must hurry home, as papa was very severe and might beat them. Major Gael left too, as he began to worry that his general might miss him.

I went to sleep. In the middle of my sleep, the door rattled violently, and Gael's fat and faithful driver tore into my room. His shirt was torn and covered with blood. He was quite out of breath and inarticulate with excitement. After some difficulty, I got his story. The major, after leaving the party, was in too happy a mood to go straight back to his division. The least he could do, he figured, was to liberate a French town. Granville, a French town of fair proportions, was only twelve miles away, and seemed a likely prospect. So he and his driver, completely alone, charged into Granville and began to engage the Germans. But they found more Germans than necessary. Gael said he would try to hold off the Germans in the darkness, and sent his driver back for reinforcements. The driver begged me to hurry if I wanted to find his major alive.

I hurried over to the 4th Armored Division. They said that Gael should be court-martialed if still alive, and that the 4th Armored had orders to bypass Granville. But they finally gave me three armored scout cars, and we reached Granville a little after dawn. We found the town in a state of intense celebration. The Tricolor and the Stars and Stripes both flew over the *mairie,* and Paul was being carried about on the shoulders of a group of FFI's. The cortege behind them was singing the "Marseillaise," and the German-inclined girls had been rounded up and the process of shaving their heads was well under way.

The turn of events was startling, but Gael explained it in a few words. During the night, while he was shooting it out with the

CHARTRES, AUGUST 18, 1944. *After the Allies had liberated the town, a group of French men and women who had collaborated with the Germans was rounded up in the courtyard of the Préfecture de Police. The women's heads were shaved; many of the men were presumably shot by firing squads.*

Overleaf: CHARTRES, AUGUST 18, 1944. *The mother of a German-fathered child, her head shaved, is marched through the streets and taunted by the townspeople. Her own mother (barely visible over the right shoulder of the man at right carrying a cloth sack) was similarly punished.*

Germans, a little man with a tremendous mustache and an old gun joined him, and led him to the hiding French Forces of the Interior. Gael took command, appointing as his chief of staff the man with the mustache. Gael swore that his little friend had fought like a lion. Altogether, they killed seventeen Germans, and captured one hundred fifty.

The festivities subsided around noon. Paul gallantly kissed both cheeks of the mustache, and the fighters of the night said farewell. We were weary and hungry, and Paul, his driver, and I started out to find a good restaurant. All the citizens of Granville agreed that our best bet was the Grand Hotel. We found the place, and it looked promising. The dining room was spotless and the tables were set. A large lady dressed in the severest black sat behind the *caisse,* surrounded by bottles of aperitifs. She cast a suspicious eye at us, let us sit down, and called the *patron.* He appeared in an immaculate white apron and an extra-tall chef's hat. He was a little man, his mustache was immense. It was Paul's hero himself. He brought us the menu, glanced at Madame, and asked brusquely, "And who is going to pay for it?"

———

Not everyone had a gay time. Patton's armor was rolling without much opposition, but the infantry had to fight hard to keep the Germans from cutting the road behind Patton.

Ernest Hemingway sent a message to me at Granville. From the start of the French campaign, he had attached himself to the 4th Infantry. He said that the infantry was having a good war for a photographer and I ought to stop fooling around behind a lot of tanks. He sent a freshly captured Mercedes, in all its luxury, to fetch me, and I unwillingly climbed in and was driven to his battlefield.

The forty-eight stitches had left no visible trace on Papa's scalp, and he had shaved off his unprintable beard. He received me crisply. He had become an honorary member of the 4th Division and was as widely respected for his guts and military knowledge as for his writing. He had a little army of his own inside the division. The commanding general, Barton, had assigned to him as public relations officer Lieutenant Stevenson, Teddy Roosevelt's former aide. He was also assigned a cook, a driver, a former motorbike champion who functioned as photographer, and his own ration of Scotch.

Officially, they were all public relations personnel, but under Papa's influence they became a bunch of bloodthirsty Indians. Hemingway, as a war correspondent, was not allowed to carry arms, but his task force carried every weapon imaginable, of both German and American make. They were even motorized. Besides the Mercedes, they had captured a motorcycle replete with sidecar.

Papa said there was an interesting attack going on a few miles away and thought we ought to investigate. We put some whisky, a few machine guns, and a bunch of hand grenades in the sidecar, and set out in the general direction of the attack.

The 8th Regiment of the 4th was supposed to retake a little town, and Papa had it all figured out. The regiment had already begun the attack, an hour earlier, from the left flank of the village, and he was sure we could take a shortcut and drive in from the right flank without much difficulty.

He showed me on the map how easy it would be, but I didn't like it at all. Papa looked at me with disgust and said I could stay behind. I couldn't do anything but follow him, but I made it clear that I was going under protest. I told him that Hungarian strategy consisted of going behind a good number of soldiers, and never of taking lonely shortcuts through no-man's-land.

We set out on the road leading to the village. Papa, his redheaded driver, and the photographer on the bike went ahead, while Lieutenant "Stevie" and I followed a good five yards behind. We advanced cautiously, consulting our map at frequent intervals. At length, we reached the last sharp curve before the road led straight into town. I didn't hear any shooting from the direction of the village, and I began to feel very uncomfortable. Papa pooh-poohed me, and I followed under even more protest. When he reached the curve, something powerful pooh-poohed ten yards away from him. It was an exploding shell. He was thrown into the air and landed in a ditch. Red and the photographer, who quickly abandoned his motorbike, retreated. The four of us were well protected on our side of the curve. Not so Papa, on his side. Besides, the ditch was shallow, and his behind stuck out at least an inch. Tracer bullets were hitting the dirt just above his head, and the popping, which came from a light German tank at the entrance to the village, continued without a letup. For two hours he was pinned down, until the Germans found a more pressing target in the form of the delayed 8th Regiment.

Now Papa ran for it and reached our side of the bend. He was furious. Not so much at the Germans as at me, and accused me of standing by during his crisis so that I might take the first picture of the famous writer's dead body.

During the evening, relations were somewhat strained between the strategist and the Hungarian military expert.

—

The road to Paris was calling. The Third Army reached Laval, some sixty miles from Paris, and I hurried to catch up with them. A little shooting here and there, a new bunch of broken-down German prisoners, another town named in the communiqués, and we arrived at Rambouillet. This was our last stop before Paris, and there we had to halt—this time for political reasons.

The people of Paris had arisen and were fighting the Germans in the streets by themselves. The Allied Supreme Command decided that under the circumstances it would be a nice touch to have the cream of De Gaulle's new army, the French Second Armored Division—fully equipped by the Americans—enter Paris as the spearhead of the army of liberation.

The French division assembled at Rambouillet and prepared for the last jump. They were a well-blended cocktail of fighting men. French marines who had won fame with Montgomery in the Libyan desert, still wearing their old sailor berets with the red pompons. Spanish Republicans and black Senegalese, Frenchmen escaped from German prison camps—they all wore the easy smile of fighters.

Every international typewriter was assembled around Rambouillet too, and every accredited war correspondent, wrangling and conspiring to be the first to enter Paris and file history from the great city of former lights.

Hemingway had taken Rambouillet long before the Free French and newspaper armies arrived. His private four-man army had enlisted some enthusiastic young men from the Resistance, and was now grown to fifteen. The mixed force took after Papa, copying his sailor bear walk, spitting short sentences from the corners of their mouths in their different languages. They carried more hand grenades and brandy than a full division. Every night they went out to harass the remaining Germans between Rambouillet and Paris. Papa had no place in his army for Hungarian experts anymore, so I rejoined Charlie Wertenbaker, who had a jeep of his own for the rush to Paris.

On the twenty-fourth of August, the French rolled up the sleeves of their tanks and were off. The night of the twenty-fifth, we bivouacked under a road sign reading: "PORTE D'ORLÉANS—6 KILO-METERS." It was the best road sign I've ever slept under.

The sun was in a hurry to rise that morning, and we did not bother to brush our teeth. The tanks were already rattling on the pavement. That happy morning, when we got on the road, even our driver, Pfc Strickland, forgot his Virginia manners and every five minutes poked my distinguished boss in the ribs.

Just two miles outside Paris, our jeep was stopped by a tank belonging to the French Second Armor. We were told we could go no further: General Leclerc had given strict orders not to let anyone but members of the French Second enter the city. The old boy was definitely losing charm. I got out of our jeep and began to argue with the men in the tank. They spoke French with a Spanish intonation. Then I noticed the name of the tank. Painted on the turret was the word "TERUEL."

In the winter of 1937, when I was with the Spanish Republicans, I was with them in one of their greatest victories, the Battle of Teruel. I spoke to the men in the tank. "*No hay derecho*—there is no justice if you stop me. I am one of *vosotros*—your very own—and I myself took part in that ferociously cold battle."

"If this is *verdad*," they answered, "and you are telling us the truth, then indeed you are one of *nosotros*, and you must come up and ride with us into Paris in this *verdadero* tank Teruel!"

I mounted the tank. Charlie and Strickland followed in the jeep.

The road to Paris was open, and every Parisian was out in the street to touch the first tank, to kiss the first man, to sing and cry. Never were there so many who were so happy so early in the morning.

PARIS, AUGUST 25, 1944. *After the entry of the French 2d Armored Division,
numerous pockets of German snipers had to be rooted out in street fighting.
Many French civilians and members of the Resistance helped the
French troops in this fighting.*

Opposite: PARIS, AUGUST 25, 1944.

PARIS, AUGUST 25–26, 1944. *A French Resistance fighter in the liberated city. Note the homemade medals.*

PARIS, AUGUST 26, 1944. *General Charles de Gaulle leads the triumphal parade down the Avenue des Champs-Elysées to celebrate the liberation of the city.*

Overleaf: PARIS, AUGUST 26, 1944. *Celebrating the liberation of the city.*

PARIS, AUGUST 26, 1944.

Left: PARIS, AUGUST 26, 1944. *When snipers in buildings overlooking the Place de l'Hôtel de Ville opened fire, the panicked crowd fell to the pavement.*

I felt that this entry into Paris had been made especially for me. On a tank made by the Americans who had accepted me, riding with the Spanish Republicans with whom I had fought against fascism long years ago, I was returning to Paris—the beautiful city where I first learned to eat, drink, and love.

The thousands of faces in the finder of my camera became more and more blurred; that finder was very very wet. We drove through the *quartier* where I had lived for six years, passed my house by the Lion of Belfort. My concierge was waving a handkerchief, and I was yelling to her from the rolling tank, *"C'est moi, c'est moi!"*

———

Our first stop was in front of the Café de Dôme in the Montparnasse. My favorite table was empty. Girls in light printed dresses climbed up on our tank and ersatz lipstick soon covered our faces. The best-looking of my Spaniards got more than his share, but he murmured, "How I would prefer to be kissed by the ugliest old woman in Madrid than by the fairest girl in Paris."

Around the Chamber of Deputies we had to fight, and some of the lipstick got washed off with blood. Late in the evening, Paris was free.

I wanted to spend my first night in the best of best hotels—the Ritz. But the hotel was already occupied. Hemingway's army had come into Paris by a different road, and after a short and happy fight had taken their main objective and liberated the Ritz from the German yokels. Red was standing guard before the entrance, happily displaying every missing front tooth. He said, in best imitation Hemingway, "Papa took good hotel. Plenty stuff in cellar. You go up quick."

It was all true. Papa made up with me, gave me a party, and the key to the best room in the hotel.

XI

The liberation of Paris was the most unforgettable day in the world. The most unforgettable day plus seven was the bluest. The food was gone, the champagne was gone, and the girls had returned to their homes to explain the facts of the liberation. The shops were closed, the streets were empty, and suddenly we realized that the war was not over. In fact, it was going on just twenty-five miles away.

On that seventh day I was sitting at the bar of the Scribe Hotel, the Army's grand gesture to the newspapermen, trying to teach Gaston to mix that most potent of pick-me-ups, the "Suffering Bastard." While he was shaking the tomato juice, vodka, and Worcestershire sauce together, I was tolling the knell for the noble art of war photography, which had expired in the streets of Paris only six days before. There would never again be pictures of dough-boys like those in the deserts of North Africa or the mountains of Italy; never again an invasion to surpass that of the Normandy beach; never a liberation to equal Paris.

I told Gaston that going back to the front was a dull prospect. From now on I would be taking the same pictures over and over again. Every crouching soldier, every rolling tank, or crowd of madly waving people would be just a kid brother of some picture I had taken somewhere before.

Gaston poured the mixture, and while I drank it he lamented over his own heroic period.

During the occupation he had fought in the Maquis down in southern France. Most of the men fighting there were exiled Spanish Republicans, and their commander a General Alvarez. They had no tanks, and only a few machine guns, but their war was never monotonous.

"Now that the south of France is liberated," said Gaston, "I have exchanged the rifle for the cocktail shaker. But the Spaniards kept their arms. Soon they will cross the Pyrenees and liberate their Spain from Franco."

I finished the drink. I felt much better all around.

———

Back in January of 1939, when the fascists took Barcelona, the hundred miles of road from Barcelona to the French border was black with people fleeing Franco's imported legions. Intellectuals and workers, peasants and shopkeepers, mothers, wives, and children, they followed and led the few remaining vehicles of the disorganized Republican Army. They carried their bundles and walked with blistered feet toward the freedom of democratic France.

The newspapermen wrote their story and I took their pictures. But the world was not very interested, and in a few short years there were many other people on many other roads, running and falling before the same troops and the very same swastikas.

The French gendarmes received the exhausted Spanish refugees with the cruel indifference of people who are warm and well fed. One by one the refugees reached the border, their exodus protected by the rear guard of the Republican Army, a few thousand soldiers who made up the Brigade of Madrid. They had fought from the first day to the very end, but when the last civilian had crossed over into France, there was nothing left for them but to cross too. Their commander, General Modesto, sat erect on a white horse at the border. The brigade marched by in the light of flickering torches. Their rifles were clean and shiny, their heads high, their eyes moist in the torchlight. Passing their general, they clenched their fists, raised their right arms, and cried, "*Ya volveremos*... we will return!"

The surprised French gendarmes automatically raised their arms and saluted. But later the entire brigade was placed in concentration camps.

—

In Toulouse, at the headquarters of the French Forces of the Interior, I was received by General Alvarez. He was young and keen and very anxious to recross that border. But he had to wait for a signal from the Allies. He felt sure it wouldn't be long in coming. The Allies had spent many lives on the roads toward Rome and Berlin. The road to Madrid would be next.

He suggested that I visit his troops. He had about twenty thousand men in all, concentrated in little border villages on the French side of the Pyrenees.

When I arrived, my Spaniards were having a big party in an old tavern. They were singing songs and drinking heavy red wine from two-necked bottles. They held the bottles high by the large neck and caught the thin stream from the narrow neck in the corners of their half-open mouths.

In the middle of the room a dark gypsy from Andalusia was singing flamenco. The others clapped their hands at the refrains and yelled *"Holé!"* Following the gypsy came a sad Catalan, who sang the melancholy *jotas* of his province. The Catalans listened with soft eyes; the others shouted *"Muy bien!"* at the end of each song. Next came a Gallego. He had the broad face of a peasant and his song had green fields and high mountains in it. He sang many such songs and after the last one they always made him sing another.

There was a lean man who never clapped and never yelled, and now he took the floor. Over his heart he wore many stripes, each for a big battle, some of them in Spain, some of them in France. He sang a song I had never heard before. The words were in Spanish, but the beautiful melody was strange to us all.

When he finished, there was silence. Then someone asked, "Tell me, *hombre*, where do they sing this song?"

"In the Valley of Aran," he replied, "only twenty miles from

TOULOUSE, NOVEMBER 1944. *A meeting of the Unión Nacional Española, an organization of antifascist Spaniards who believed that since they had helped to liberate France, the Allies now had a responsibility to help them liberate Spain from Generalissimo Franco. The Allies felt no such sense of responsibility.*

here—on the other side of the mountain. It is a small valley and there are only three villages. They are surrounded by tremendous mountains and isolated almost as much from Spain as from France. That is where they sing this song, and that is where my Novia has waited for me these many years."

A bearded man with rank on his shoulders arose. "I am the commander of the frontier post on the Col d'Aran. I suggest we go to this valley."

There was immediate agreement. The men in the tavern volunteered to cross the mountains and visit the place where the songs were so beautiful and where a Novia had been waiting six years for a man who was only twenty miles away.

They telephoned headquarters at Toulouse for permission. But General Alvarez said no, it was impossible. The men became very subdued. The barrel which had nourished the bottles was dry anyway, and the party began to break up.

Then headquarters called back. This time permission was granted. "One hundred and fifty men may cross the border. They are to avoid bloodshed and are to return to France within twenty-four hours. They are to find out how the Spaniards feel about their exiled brothers, and to learn whether they know that the Spaniards in France have been continuing the fight against the fascists."

As for the *Americano*, I was to stay. Headquarters said I might go only as far as the border post, lest I create an international situation.

We climbed aboard trucks, a hundred-odd men in all, and drove cautiously along a winding road, eight thousand feet up in the mountains. The border post was a little wooden shack, and there we dismounted. A narrow path led into the clouds hanging at the top of the mountain. On the other side was Spain.

I stayed behind with the bearded post commander. The others shouldered their rifles, set out in Indian file, and disappeared into the mist.

———

Inside the shack, we made a big fire, brewed some strong coffee, and waited. At 11:00 A.M. Radio Madrid interrupted a program for an important announcement: "Ten thousand criminals of Spanish origin, carrying American arms and wearing French uniforms, have crossed the border from communist France. The nearest detachments of the Army and Falange have been alerted and are expected to engage them shortly."

The bearded man said that Franco was from bad milk and was born with a lie in his mouth. The guards agreed. Then the French radio made a special announcement of its own: "All Spaniards who fought with the FFI will be moved at least twenty miles away from the border. Those who crossed over to Spain will be disarmed and interned upon their return." The commander muttered something about the milk of the French. We were all very worried.

In a little while French military trucks filled with regular French soldiers drove up to the post. They ordered the commander and his guards to withdraw immediately and report back to Toulouse. I stayed on with the French. Evening fell, but none of the Spaniards returned. An argument developed around the fire. Some of the French complained that those damn foreigners were always causing trouble. Others remembered that those damn foreigners had fought damn well against the Germans, and had liberated some of the villages where they themselves lived. But they all agreed that the Spaniards would have to be interned as ordered.

At midnight the guard came in, his uniform covered with snow. The French captain said that it was too bad, but the Spaniards had asked for it. They would have wet, frozen feet when they crossed the col higher up. But they did not come, only thick snowflakes drifted in during the night.

In the morning there was two feet of virgin snow on the ground. It was still snowing, and the French said it would be impossible now to cross the pass.

But at 10:00 A.M. a thin shadow in the mist slowly approached the shack, making deep holes in the snow where once the path had been. He was alone and he carried six rifles on his shoulder. The French guard stopped him, and he surrendered his rifles and said he was ready. The French captain was very uneasy. He swore under his breath and said it wasn't right to arrest a man who had brought six rifles through that storm. They told him to disappear quickly and dry

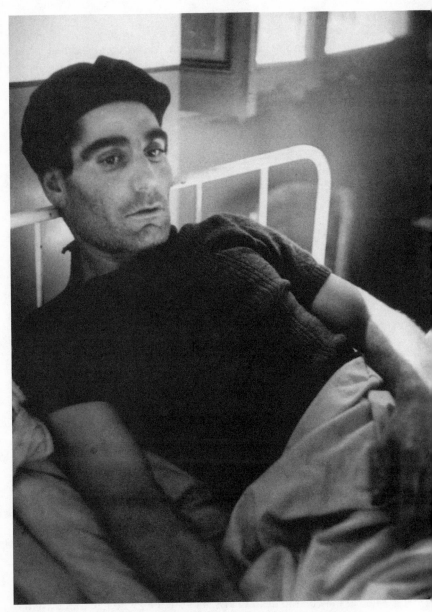

NEAR TOULOUSE, NOVEMBER 1944. *A Spanish antifascist exiled in France. He had been a member of the abortive mission that had crossed the Pyrenees on foot in October 1944 to liberate several Spanish villages.*

his feet down in the village. The Spaniard started to go, then looked back toward the top of the mountain and said, "*Creo que hay otros*... I think there may be others." Then he walked slowly away.

The next one carried a wounded comrade on his back. They could not arrest those two either. By noon thirty-seven in all had returned, all of them men too good and in too pitiful a condition to be interned.

Gradually we got their story. When they came down from the mountain into Spain the night before, the whole village turned out to greet them. The priest said that the village knew about their fight and was praying for them. A tremendous table was laid and they ate bread, drank wine, and danced. Suddenly one of them warned that the Falange from the next garrison was coming. They beat an orderly retreat, but when they began to climb toward the col, they were surprised by the sudden snow. They were able to make slow progress and the white snow made them easy targets for the rifles of the Falange. Most of the men were hit, and their frozen bodies stayed behind in the Spanish snow.

The last man to arrive at the post was accompanied by two boys. He was the lean man with the strange song, and his mouth was now a thin line. The boys stumbling behind him were in the uniform of Franco's Falange. The lean man came to the fire and made the boys take off their shoes and rub their feet.

I made him drink from my flask, and in a broken voice he told me his story. These were the young brothers of his Novia, and they had been made to join the Falange. The girl and the boys came along with him when they were forced to retreat. Midway up the hill they had to make their choice. The boys wanted to enlist in the French Army and fight the Germans. So Novia returned to the village to care for her mother... and continue to wait for perhaps many more years to come.

The road back to Spain is a long one. That ugly old woman in Madrid may be too dead to kiss, and the men who live to return may be too old to be kissed by the young ones.

XII

Back at the Hotel Scribe, the doorman said that someone was waiting for me in the bar—indeed, had been waiting for three whole days. Behind the bar Gaston was mixing a drink for a young American major. It was Chris with a promotion.

Even from a distance he looked like the beginning of a beautiful hangover. I pulled up a stool and sat down beside him. He saw me through the bottom of his glass and set it down. "It's about time," he said. "Come on, we're going back to London."

The last letters from London had indeed hinted at a Pink uprising, but that wasn't any reason for Chris to get his teeth floating so early in the day. "Where's the ultimatum?" I demanded.

"Pinky's through sending you letters. It's no use, she says. Now that your Paris is free again, you don't care about what you've left behind in England."

I couldn't go back to England now; it was impossible. I explained that I would have to get a visa from the British, and that I would have to receive Army orders in order to get on a plane. All that would take many days. Besides, I had to go back to the front. Pinky would simply have to wait.

But Chris insisted. "It's all fixed," he told me. "I've borrowed the general's plane; and, as for the security chaps on the field, just leave them to me. There won't be a hitch. I've even arranged for a plane to bring you back tomorrow morning."

No, it was still no good, I answered. Pinky had given up our apartment; and if I sneaked into London illegally, I wouldn't be able to register in a hotel.

Chris overruled me. "Pinky's moved into the Dorchester. Besides, she's really in bad shape, and you've got to go. I can't keep the plane much longer."

The general's plane was on the field, and the pilot helped us in. On the plane Chris passed out, and I began to worry. The war was nearly over, and I didn't want any more passport troubles.

It was almost dark when we landed at Northolt, twenty miles from London, and by then Chris was revived. Passing through the security people, Chris pushed me ahead and told them in a low voice that I had V.O.C.G. In the jeep, Chris confided that it wasn't infectious. It meant simply "Verbal Orders Commanding General."

———

Once in town, we called up the Dorchester. Pinky was in. She was all ready and waiting, and asked us to meet her at the Astor Club, near the hotel.

She was wearing the same black dress and black sandals as at the Yardleys' eighteen months earlier, but now she was thin and pale. She kissed Chris lightly on the cheek and told him he was a good boy. Then she turned to me.

"It's time you came back."

"I shouldn't be here at all."

"Why didn't you answer my letters?"

"Let's dance."

We danced a little, mostly stood in the middle of the floor. Chris was watching us from the side.

"Be nice to Chris," Pinky said. "He's in love."

"Can't you leave even children alone?"

"Don't worry; he loves you much more than he loves me."

Chris cut in, saying something about the junior prom. He's a good dancer and they made an elegant pair. Back at the table, we drank a bottle of champagne. Pinky stood in the middle of the floor with me once more, danced twice more with Chris. A little after midnight Chris got up, saying that my plane was due to leave at nine in the morning, and that he'd pick me up at seven sharp in front of the Dorchester.

We stayed a little while longer, then left. In front of her hotel, Pinky gave me the key to room 403. "You'd better go in alone," she said. "I'll be along shortly. Walk straight to the lift. Don't hesitate, and don't look toward the desk."

I did as she directed. But while I was waiting for the elevator, a big man came toward me. He had small eyes and a waxed red mustache, and was dressed in a shiny blue suit. I acted easy and stared right past his eyes on the point of his mustache. It didn't work.

"I beg your pardon. Are you registered, sir?" There was no benefit of doubt in his tone.

"Well, not exactly," I answered. "I'm going up to see Miss Parker."

Miss Parker had no sitting room, he told me, so she couldn't very well receive visitors, besides she was not at home, besides he was the hotel detective. I stuttered something and retreated out of the hotel. Pinky was just coming in. "Coward," she accused.

We crossed Park Lane and were in Hyde Park. Our feet sank in the wet leaves. Pinky kept her hands in her pockets.

"In a few hours you'll be back to your war."

"I have to go."

"You'll have another one of your funny stories to tell."

I could not answer, not even in the dark.

"I'm no longer pretty. Now if you leave me, I'll pine away."

I objected. "You're very pretty."

"I don't want to live when I grow ugly."

We passed the dark bulk of the Dorchester again, and the faint light trickled under the front door. "The war will not last much longer," I answered lamely.

"For you it will never last long enough."

We walked again in the wet grass. Pinky's stockings were soaked above her ankles and her sandals were covered with mud. We passed by the Marble Arch and stopped before an arrow pointing to an air-raid shelter. We walked down. The steel cots were still occupied. The tired gray faces of the bombed-out Cockneys did not relax in sleep. Husbands and wives slept in separate bunks; children were squeezed together in one. The warden approached us and asked for our shelter tickets. Pinky told him she just wanted to show her American friend the other London, and we turned back to the park.

The naked trees were crying in the fog. The night was graying and we passed the Dorchester many times. Then I asked Pinky to come over and join me in Paris. "You can borrow a war correspondent's uniform from one of the girl reporters on *Life*," I said. "And Chris can smuggle you over." The controls at the Orly airfield near Paris weren't very strict, I explained, and once she arrived in Paris in an American uniform, no one would ask her for permits or passports.

She was silent for a while. Then she suggested that we get some breakfast.

At the Lyon's Corner House she took off her shoes and dried her stockings on the radiator. She bent down to put them on again. Without looking up, she asked, "Do you really want me to come?"

I assured her that I did.

"Yes, it's possible," she said. "You have guts enough to jump out of a plane with a parachute on your back, but you're scared of a little hotel detective and scared to death of falling in love. I'll come to Paris."

She powdered her face, poured the tea, and began to bubble. She became a different Pinky. She wanted to know whether she'd be able to buy any Arpège, whether she'd have occasion to wear an evening gown, whether she should bring a typewriter to go with her uniform, and where we'd live. I said yes to everything and described the comforts of the Hotel Lancaster.

The tea and toast were cold, but the breakfast was very gay.

At 7 A.M. we found Chris at the door of the wakening Dorchester. He looked green, and said he'd slept in his car. Pinky kissed me good-bye and disappeared through the revolving doors. In the car I told Chris about our night, and he promised to bring Pinky over to Paris soon.

He V.O.C.G.'d me through the controls again and put me aboard a courier plane. Before leaving, he said that V.O.C.G. really meant "Very Ordinary Capa Going." Then he added, "I hope there are no hotel dicks in Paris."

I told him he was getting on my goat.

XIII

Behind the empty bar, Gaston was reading his newspaper. The formidable General Patton was on the offensive again and had crossed the river Saar into Germany. Gaston said that this was a thing of great importance, and added that every real newspaperman was already off to the front.

Over at the Paris *Life* office, I found a stack of cables for me. They were from my boss in New York. He shared Gaston's feelings, and urged me to join Patton's army. So I packed my bag and returned to the Big War. Now that we were fighting in Germany proper, I hoped my pictures would be exciting again, and maybe a little different from those of the past campaigns.

I joined the 80th Division at the Saar River. Two battalions were already across the river in Germany, and the Germans were concentrating their heavy artillery on the small bridgehead. Most of the stuff was falling around the pontoon bridges, without which the two battalions could not be supplied with food or ammunition.

In the valley of the Saar I found a new secret weapon: artificial fog released from barrels. The stuff covered the entire area, and made it impossible for anyone to see more than two yards in front of his nose. The fog was being generated by a battalion of Negroes operating under steady fire. Black men and white men alike became gray silhouettes in the transforming vapor. I stopped to talk with one of the Negroes. Those exploding shells were talking to him, he said, each with a special message. A shell fell close by, and he grinned. "That one sounded like 'You ain't goin' back to Alabama.'"

The smoke of the shells thickened the fog still further, but the GI's went undisturbed about their business. My jeep moved slowly across the crowded bridge. I seemed to be the only one scared, but I was very glad to be back at the front.

On the other side of the Saar I located battalion headquarters in the cellar of a small building. For the next few days it became my home. The artificial fog made it impossible to take pictures anyway, and I was convinced that the Army had invented the stuff not only against the enemy but against photographers too. I found a copy of *War and Peace*, and for five days and five nights I lay on my bedroll reading Tolstoy by the light of my torch.

It was a bad place for any man, and a hopeless one for a photographer, but my bedroll was warm and the book made great reading. As for the sound effects, they seemed made to order.

Down in our cellar, we were separated from the outside world; our war was fought in the streets around our house. We paid little attention to the daily communiqué about the other fronts until we received a special bulletin announcing that Von Runstedt and the Germans had broken through our lines and were advancing toward Liége. At first we did not believe it, but then the radio confirmed it. I left *War and Peace* unfinished in the cellar, and recrossed the Saar.

Headquarters of the 12th Army Group at Verdun was in a great stew. The Germans were still advancing, and we had only three divisions in reserve to hold them back until we were able to regroup our armies. Those were the three airborne divisions; one of them was already surrounded and cut off, although still resisting in a little town

Overleafs: SOUTH OF BASTOGNE, BELGIUM, DECEMBER 23–26, 1944. *U.S. infantry crossing a frozen field during the Battle of the Bulge, and a German tank hit by American fighter planes.*

called Bastogne. It was the 101st Airborne, and it became one of the great stories of the war.

Army Intelligence was a bit touchy about the German offensive. According to their reports, those German armies either had been annihilated or were over on the eastern front. Now Intelligence refused to part with any information. Everything was top secret. I received a tip, however, from Colonel Redding, the chief PRO. If I was interested in Bastogne, he said, I ought to look for the 4th Armored Division. He provided me with a jeep, and I lit off in the general direction of Bastogne.

Every few miles we were stopped by special MP's. They carefully examined our orders and identification cards, and asked for the ever-changing password. Then, when we gave the password, they insisted on asking me a lot of very foolish and very embarrassing questions. "What is the capital of Nebraska?" they wanted to know; and "Who won the last World Series?" They explained that German spies and saboteurs were being dropped by parachute behind our communication lines, and were now promenading around in American uniforms and speaking perfect English. I spoke far from perfect English, and my accent seemed a bit unfashionable. What was worse, I did not know the capital of Nebraska. I was arrested a number of times, each time being delayed for many hours.

Finally we reached the headquarters of the 4th Armored Division, only about twenty miles from Bastogne. Their tanks were pushing ahead to relieve the airborne troops, who were a pretty battered bunch by now, and very short of ammunition.

I checked in as usual over at Intelligence. But no sooner did I tell the colonel that I was a photographer than I was placed under arrest. I was put in a corner and ordered to turn my face to the wall—so that I could not see the situation maps. They finally got Colonel Redding on the phone, and I was allowed to turn around. The Intelligence officer did not bother to say he was sorry; this was no time to be an enemy alien.

———

It was two days before Christmas. The fields were covered with snow and the temperature was well below zero. With frozen hands and

SOUTH OF BASTOGNE, BELGIUM, DECEMBER 23–26, 1944. *An American soldier captures a German.*

SOUTH OF BASTOGNE, BELGIUM, DECEMBER 23–26, 1944.
A farmer buries his horse.

feet, with weeping eyes, we pushed day and night to relieve Bastogne and bring the Christmas turkey to the boys of the 101st. Of the many correspondents on the drive, I was the only photographer. I wore all my clothes and over them I wore a long parka with a fur hood—something I had borrowed the year before from the mountain commandos on the Italian front.

My icy cameras hung around my neck, and I could not keep my gloved hand on the frozen shutter for longer than a split second. Five miles from Bastogne, I stopped my jeep on the road. A battalion of infantry was advancing on the snow-covered field just off the road. The smoke of the exploding shells hung above the black figures who were alternately lying down and standing up on the white carpet. It was my first unusual picture of war in a long time. I climbed up on the embankment, took my Contax with the longest lens, and began to shoot. Suddenly a GI from the infantry battalion, about 150 yards away, yelled something to me and raised his tommy gun at the same time. I yelled back, "Take it easy!" but as he heard my accent he began to shoot. For a fraction of a moment I didn't know what to do. If I threw myself flat on the snow he still could hit me. If I ran down the embankment, he would run after me. I threw my hands high in the air, yelled *"Kamerad!"* and surrendered. Three of them came at me with raised rifles. When they were close enough to make out the three German cameras around my neck, they became very happy GI's. Two Contax cameras and one Rolleiflex—I was the jackpot! I still kept my hands as high as I could, but when they were a rifle's length away from me, I asked one of them to search my breast pocket. He took out my identification and the special photographer pass signed by Eisenhower himself. "I should have shot the bastard before!" he groaned. The famous Sad Sack was a gay blade compared to my three captors. I let my hands drop, took their picture, and promised it would appear in *Life* magazine.

I rejoined the tanks. I felt safer riding with a driver who spoke with a Texas drawl.

It was Christmas Eve and the sky was full of stars. We stopped for the night and dismounted, forming little groups around our frozen tanks. I passed around my silver flask, and the cold brandy warmed our stomachs. Huddled close together the men who during the day had been killing Germans and shooting at accents began to sing "Stille Nacht, Heilige Nacht." Then suddenly, like the star of Bethlehem, a bright star burst in the sky and stayed right over Bastogne. It was a flare from a German plane; the Luftwaffe was delivering its presents to the 101st Division. We used unprintable language and remounted our tanks.

On the three roads to Bastogne the three wise colonels who led the three combat teams carrying presents of tinned food and shells saw the star and began moving.

The combat team with which I rode was commanded by Lieutenant Colonel Abrams. He looked like a cigar-smoking Jewish king, and swore that he would be first to reach the town.

Late next afternoon, after much fighting, we reached a hilltop. Bastogne lay below us, only three thousand yards and two thousand Germans away. Abrams lined up his tanks side by side and ordered a charge. He told his men to keep on going and keep on shooting, without stopping to aim, until they reached the town below.

McAuliffe, the commander of the 101st, the general who had said "Nuts!" to the Germans when they asked him to surrender, was quite polite. "It's good to see you, colonel," he greeted Abrams. He wasn't kidding.

On the black, charred walls of an abandoned barn, scrawled in white chalk, was the legend of McAuliffe's GI's: KILROY WAS STUCK HERE.

XIV

SPRING 1945

On the snow-covered fields of Paris, the GI's fought the French mademoiselles with snowballs. The last German offensive was beaten; the last winter of the war was waiting for the coming of the last spring.

I was waiting for Pinky.

Elmer Lower, the wily head of *Life*'s Paris office, invited me over to a small conference. He had two cables on his desk. One of them was from the New York office, saying that Bastogne was a great story, and that as a reward I could take my pick of the four American armies for the drive on Berlin. The other cable was from the London office, from the head of the accounting department, saying that he had long refused to approve poker losses as items on my expense account; now he definitely would not approve a girl's war correspondent uniform, for which a bill had been submitted by my tailor.

Elmer had some interesting information of his own. Besides the four American armies already in the field, a fifth one—the First Allied Airborne Army—was being prepared, and it was rumored that the war would end with the airborne troops jumping right into Berlin. He said that this triple-A army would take along only three war correspondents: one newspaperman, one radio commentator, and one photographer. The members of the picture pool had all agreed I could have the job. Elmer said he didn't want to push me to jump, but if I liked the idea, he had nothing against my staying in Paris until the thing came off.

Sixty days of Pinking and one day of jumping seemed like a good deal—at least it would seem so until the fifty-ninth day. I accepted the assignment, and wired London to pay the indiscreet tailor out of my salary.

The next office cable from London had a brief personal message for me: PROCAPA EXPINKY HOTEL LANCASTER FIFTEENTH OF FEBRU-ARY. For the time being, I stayed on in the hotel reserved for the war correspondents, the Scribe, but reserved the two best rooms at the Lancaster starting from the fifteenth.

D-Day came, and I prepared the beachhead with flowers and champagne. I waited there all day. Late in the evening I realized I would have to smell the flowers and drink the champagne alone. In fact, this ridiculous show of manly eagerness went on for many days with the same result. On the twentieth, the daily office cable from London had another procapa-expinky clause in it: GIVE UP LAN-CASTER FOR NOW DO NOT COME TO LONDON UNDER ANY CIRCUM-STANCES EXPLANATION FOLLOWS. I paid the bill for the flowers and the champagne, and moved back to the Scribe.

Gaston remarked that I was not happy. He now served only very bad brandy, but he was a great and just barman. I made a speech about women in general and also in particular. Gaston said simply, "Monsieur ought to go and do a little winter sport."

The idea of the lonely, pipe-smoking man in the high mountains appealed to me. Besides, I knew a very pretty French girl who had left for Mégève, up in the French Alps, only a few days earlier.

I said good-bye to Elmer Lower. I told him I had made a bad deal, and when the day came he could send me a telegram to Mégève. Then I spent the next thirty days fighting against the snow, and learning the French technique of skiing. I slept well with a bottle full of hot water.

It was spring when Elmer's telegram arrived. Now was the time for every skier to jump. I was brown and healthy enough to be a coward, but I returned to Paris. There was no letter from Pinky, and Gaston advised, "Monsieur should go back to war." He was a very well-informed barman.

—

The beginning of the end, the great airborne invasion of Germany, started out in French boxcars dating from the First War and bearing the well-known inscription of *"40 hommes et 8 chevaux."* The U.S. 17th Airborne Division was packed in long freight trains, and for forty-eight hours we were shuffled all over France. This was to deceive the enemy spies. After two days of this hocus-pocus, our generals decided that both the troops and the German spies were quite tired enough, and we arrived at an enclosed camp next to an airfield, sixty miles from the spot from which we started.

At the camp, we had a short time left for the usual preinvasion cleaning of rifles and consciences. The day before the jump, we were briefed and told that we would be jumping—together with an English airborne division—on the other side of the Rhine, right in the heart of the main German defense line.

Before their battles, the old Huns and Greeks used to sacrifice white horses and other expensive animals. That afternoon, the U.S. airborne soldiers sacrificed most of their hair, shaving it off in Indian fashion. They said they preferred to be alive and hairless next evening, than dead with a full growth. I kept my hair on, but felt very thirsty. Jumping with a parachute is the greatest cure for a hangover, and it would be a waste not to have one. But there was no liquor. The 17th Airborne was a hairless, drinkless division.

Just before darkness a small cub plane circled over our camp and landed right in the middle. It was Major Chris Scott. The 9th Troop Carrier Command was once again flying us on our mission, and Chris was still in charge of the news. He had just come from London, and he had a package and a message for me from Pinky. The package contained a bottle of Scotch, and Chris told me a long story.

On the fifteenth of February, he began, the 9th TCC held a big dance at its headquarters near Leicester, in England. Chris invited Pinky with her suitcase. After the dance, he planned to hide Pinky and put her on the plane to Paris early in the morning.

The dance was a great success, and Pinky was the center of attraction. As soon as the dance was over, Pinky changed into her war correspondent's uniform, and they walked out on the airfield. Unfortunately, one of the boys who had danced with Pinky saw her on the field in her American uniform, and called up the local police.

Pinky was arrested before she could board the plane. She didn't want to give Chris away or involve me, so she told a cock and pink story which no one believed. They decided she was a spy, and for many long days she sat under glaring lights, telling the same unconvincing story.

Finally she was released, but was continually tailed. That was when she called up *Life* and asked them to send me a message, saying I was not to come to England. She couldn't very well write any of those things in a censored letter, and so Chris had flown over twice to tell me the story. But I was away skiing.

Now, Chris concluded, Pinky was back home with her parents. She sent me the bottle with her love.

Chris was obviously suffering while he told me this sad story. I asked him if he was very much in love with her. "Yes," he answered. "I've been wanting to talk with you for some time now, but Pinky made me promise not to."

I told him to go ahead and talk. "No," he said. "Tomorrow you're going to jump, and I'm going to fly in a Fortress above your formation, with some photographers who are going to take pictures of the jump. We'll meet the next night. I'll wait for you at the first airfield this side of the Rhine. That will be a better time to talk things over."

We agreed. We drank half the bottle of Scotch, and I poured the other half into my battle flask.

—

From North Africa to the Rhine there were too many D-Days, and for every one of them we had to get up in the middle of the night. The end of darkness always brought the beginning of death. But this

ARRAS, FRANCE, MARCH 23, 1945. *An American paratrooper, sporting a Mohawk for luck and esprit de corps, ready to board a plane for the jump across the Rhine.*

invasion was different. We ate our double portions of preinvasion fresh eggs at seven in the morning, and took off shortly afterwards.

I flew in the lead plane with the regimental commander, and I was to be number two man in the jump right behind him. Before boarding the plane, the G-2 major had taken me aside. If anything happened to the Old Man when we got the signal to jump, I was instructed to boot him through the door. It was a very important and comforting feeling.

Our planes flew low over France. Through the open door of the plane the boys watched the landscape of a now peaceful France pass quickly by. Nobody puked, this was a very different invasion.

Thousands of planes and gliders had taken off simultaneously from fields in England and France, and we rendezvoused over Belgium. From there on we flew together in tight formation. Our shadows traveled on the roads and streets of the liberated countries, and we could see the faces of the people waving to us. Even the dogs were fascinated, and ran after our shadows. On both sides of us were planes towing gliders, and it looked as if someone had spun strings from the Channel to the Rhine, and then had hung from them, at intervals of a hundred yards, a lot of toy airplanes.

I did not like to see or think more. I put on an act and began to read a mystery story. At 10:15 I was only up to page sixty-seven, and the red light came on to get ready. For a moment I had the foolish idea of saying, "Sorry, I cannot jump. I have to finish my story."

I stood up, made sure that my cameras were well strapped to my legs and that my flask was in my breast pocket over my heart. We still had fifteen minutes before the jump. I started to think over my whole life. It was like a movie where the projection machine has gone crazy, and I saw and felt everything I ever ate, ever did, and got to the end in twelve minutes flat. I felt very empty, I still had three minutes to go. I was standing in the open door behind the colonel. Six hundred feet below us was the Rhine. Then bullets began to hit our plane like pebbles. The green light flashed on and I did not have to kick the colonel. The boys yelled "Umbriago!" I counted one thousand, two thousand, three thousand, and up above me was the lovely sight of my open parachute. The forty seconds to earth were hours on my grandfather clock, and I had plenty of time to unstrap my camera, take a few pictures, and think of six or seven different things before I hit the ground. On the ground I kept clicking my shutter. We lay flat on the earth and nobody wanted to get up. The first fear was over, and we were reluctant to begin the second.

Ten yards away were tall trees, and some of the men who had jumped after me had landed in them, and now were hanging helplessly fifty feet from the good earth.

A German machine gun opened up at the dangling men. I began a long, loud Hungarian swear, and buried my head in the grass. A boy lying near me looked up.

"Stop those Jewish prayers," he called. "They won't help you now."

I rolled on my back, and right above us was only one plane, Chris's silver Fortress. It turned, dipped its wings gaily, and suddenly burst into flames. The smoking plane was losing altitude. "That Chris," I thought. "He's going to double-cross me and become a hero." Then, just before the plane disappeared behind the trees, I saw seven black dots—seven black dots transforming into seven silken flowers. They had jumped; their chutes were open.

At 11:00 A.M. I had two rolls of film taken, and I lit a cigarette. At 11:30 I took the first swig from my flask. We were firmly established on the other side of the Rhine. Our regiment had gotten the guns out of the wrecked gliders, and we reached the road which we were supposed to occupy and hold. We lost many of our men, but this was easier than Salerno or Anzio or Normandy. The Germans of those campaigns could have murdered us here, but these Germans were beaten. In the afternoon we made our junction with the other regiments. I closed my cameras. I had enough pictures, and began to look for Chris.

Overleafs: NEAR WESEL, GERMANY, MARCH 24, 1945.
American paratroopers make their descent. Some of the paratroopers are caught in trees as they land, making them easy targets for the enemy.

Opposite: NEAR WESEL, GERMANY, MARCH 24, 1945.

NEAR WESEL, GERMANY, MARCH 24, 1945.
A German farm family seeks refuge in a shallow foxhole.

Overleaf: NEAR WESEL, GERMANY, MARCH 24, 1945.
German farmers flee their burning house at the height of the fighting.

In the evening I began making my way toward the Rhine, but we were still cut off from the army crossing the river on barges. I found a nice big silk parachute, rolled myself in it, and went to sleep. The silk was warm and my dream was rolling on a telegraph ticker. "Go back skiing, go back skiing," it repeated, and was signed sometimes Pinky, sometimes *Life* magazine.

In the morning I reached the Rhine. Two pontoon bridges were built across the river and thousands of guns and soldiers were moving across. They all asked how the jump had been, and I told a very cocky story. They didn't mind.

I found the airfield, and inquired if they knew anything about Major Scott. "He was brought in with a broken ankle," the flight officer told me, "and was evacuated to London half an hour ago."

From the Rhine to the Oder the shooting war quickly changed into a looting war. The GI's fought their way ahead, meeting less and less resistance and finding more and more cameras, Lüger pistols, and frauleins. Advancing into the heart of Germany, they found that the Germans were a very clean people. And the houses and farms were more like the ones they had left at home than any they had seen in the earlier campaigns.

The war was not yet over, but the fraternization began. Only those who liberated the concentration camps at Buchenwald and Belsen and Dachau—they alone did not fraternize with the frauleins. The war was petering out in a confused anticlimax, and the soldiers were mentally packing their bags for home while they were still shooting their last shots.

From the Rhine to the Oder I took no pictures. The concentration camps were swarming with photographers, and every new picture of horror served only to diminish the total effect. Now, for a short day, everyone will see what happened to those poor devils in those camps; tomorrow, very few will care what happens to them in the future.

The Germans, now sullen, now suddenly friendly, didn't interest my camera either. I wanted to meet the first Russian, and then pack up my war.

The Russians were fighting in Berlin. Other Russians reached the

Oder at the same time the Americans arrived at the gates of the ruins called Leipzig. Around Leipzig we had one more hard battle. The town was defended by the elite of Hitler's storm troopers. But they, like the others, yelled *"Kamerad"* once they had killed enough Americans and had had enough themselves.

I was with a battalion of the 5th Infantry Division. We reached a bridge leading into the center of town. The first platoons were already crossing it, and we were very afraid it was going to be blown up any minute by the Germans. A fashionable four-story apartment building stood on the corner overlooking the bridge, and I climbed up to the fourth floor to see if the last picture of crouching and advancing infantrymen could be the last picture of war for my camera. The bourgeois apartment on the fourth floor was open. Five GI's belonging to a heavy-weapons company were putting up a machine gun to cover the advance over the bridge. It was hard to shoot from the window, so the sergeant and one of his men moved the gun out onto the open, unprotected balcony. I watched them from the door. When the gun had been set up, the sergeant returned. The young corporal pulled the trigger and began to shoot.

The last man shooting the last gun was not much different from the first. By the time the picture got to New York, no one would want to publish the picture of a simple soldier shooting an ordinary gun. But the boy had a clean, open, very young face, and his gun was still killing fascists. I stepped out onto the balcony and, standing about two yards away, focused my camera on his face. I clicked my shutter, my first picture in weeks—and the last one of the boy alive.

Silently, the tense body of the gunner relaxed, and he slumped and fell back into the apartment. His face was not changed except for a tiny hole between his eyes. The puddle of blood grew beside his fallen head, and his pulse had long stopped beating.

The sergeant felt his wrist, stepped over his body, and grabbed the machine gun. But he could not shoot anymore; our men had arrived at the other side of the bridge.

I had the picture of the last man to die. The last day, some of the best ones die. But those alive will fast forget.

———

We stopped in Leipzig. The do's were over and the don't's began. The Army had to stay and wait for further orders, while the newspapermen were warned not to try and get to Berlin or meet the Russian Army only fifteen miles away. From now on everything had to be done the bureaucratic way. The Army promised they would organize a meeting ceremony with the Russians—especially for generals and newspapermen.

We sent our last stories and waited around the press headquarters of the U.S. First Army. Most of the war correspondents were there. Those who had followed the war all the way from North Africa, and many new ones too. The new ones wrote fantastic stories with a great display of enthusiasm. But the old-timers were quiet, nursing the hangover of war, and their last drinks.

The first night in Leipzig we went to bed early. At midnight Hal Boyle, the most indefatigable of the old-timers, woke us up. He said, "Ernie got it." Far away from us, Ernie Pyle was killed that day on Ie Shima. We all got up and drank ourselves stupid in silence.

———

There were a lot of war correspondents who had arrived from London and Paris for the historic meeting with the Russians. One of them, with Columbia Broadcasting, asked whether Chris Scott wasn't a friend of mine. I said yes, how was he? He answered that Chris was in London, still limping, and getting ready to get himself married to an English girl.

I no longer cared to meet the Russians. The CBS man gave me the key to his London apartment, and I took a German Ford and drove straight to Paris. There I asked for orders and visas, and cabled Pinky I was coming.

XV

I paid the taxi before Pinky's home, and as I opened the door I saw her. She was waiting for me outside.

"You had to come now," she said. "Do you want to spoil everything again?" She wore glasses, looked quite well, and her voice was different. I stared at her and she said, "I got you a room at the Dorchester." I hailed another cab and we got in. I gave the driver the address of the CBS apartment over on Portland Square.

Up in the apartment, she sat down in a big chair, while I stood by the cold fireplace. Neither of us said anything. After some time, she took off her glasses and spoke in her old voice.

"Now that I see you, you don't look any different."

"I'm just the same. I haven't changed."

"I am not the same. These last two years, you've been having yourself a time, but I had only a wait. Now I am in love—and am loved too."

I said it couldn't be. It was all due to her intensity, to the stupidities of wars and passports, to the gremlins which had been following us around. "We still have our first day two years ago...and many more to come."

"Why didn't you talk this way before?"

I had no answer. "He is too young for you," I said finally.

"Now I have a beautiful dream. Why do you want to destroy it?"

Again I was silent.

"Besides," Pinky added, "Chris is no spinach."

We made a fire in the fireplace, and then I went looking to see where CBS hid its liquor. I returned with two bottles. We sat by the fire and drank, and gradually we began to talk more freely. We sat and talked and did not eat or sleep. I argued and I pleaded, and I cursed and begged, and almost beat her. She wept and argued back, and stood for it all.

The light beyond our windows changed many times, and the second morning found us sitting on the floor, surrounded by empty bottles and a dying fire. Pinky was haggard and very beautiful, and I thought I was winning her back. I said I would go shave, and then we would have some breakfast.

While I was shaving, I heard her talking on the phone. When I came out of the bathroom, Pinky had her overcoat on, her face was made up, and she wore her glasses. She said, "I want to kiss you." Then she walked out. In front of the door there were two bottles of milk and two newspapers. The letters on the top paper were unusually fat:

WAR IN EUROPE OVER

There is absolutely no reason to get up in the mornings any more.

Appendix

The following photographers, working in the Capa tradition, have received the Robert Capa Award, a medal that has been given annually since 1955 by *Life* magazine and the Overseas Press Club of America "for superlative photography requiring exceptional courage and enterprise abroad."

1955 Howard Sochurek
1956 John Sadovy
1957 No Award
1958 Paul Bruck
1959 Mario Biasetti
1960 Yung Su Kwan
1961 No Award
1962 Peter Dehmel and Klaus Dehmel
1963 Larry Burrows
1964 Horst Faas
1965 Larry Burrows
1966 Henri Huet
1967 David Douglas Duncan
1968 John Olson
1969 Anonymous Czech photographer
      (Given secretly to protect the photographer,
      Josef Koudelka)

1970 Kyoichi Sawada (posthumously)
1971 Larry Burrows (posthumously)
1972 Clive W. Limpkin
1973 David Burnett, Raymond Depardon, and Charles Gerretsen
1974 W. Eugene Smith
1975 Dirck Halstead
1976 Catherine Leroy
1977 Eddie Adams
1978 Susan Meiselas
1979 Kaveh Golestan
1980 Steve McCurry
1981 Rudi Frey
1982 Harry Mattison
1983 James Nachtwey
1984 James Nachtwey
1985 Peter Magubane
1986 James Nachtwey
1987 Janet Knott
1988 Chris Steele Perkins
1989 David Turnley
1990 Bruce Haley
1991 Christopher Morris
1992 Luc Delahaye
1993 Paul Watson
1994 James Nachtwey
1995 Anthony Suau
1996 Corrine Dufka
1997 Horst Faas and Tim Page for *Requiem*
1998 James Nachtwey

BIBLIOGRAPHY

BOOKS BY ROBERT CAPA

Death in the Making. Photographs by Robert Capa and Gerda Taro. Captions by Robert Capa, translated by Jay Allen. Preface by Jay Allen. Layout by André Kertész. New York: Covici, Friede, 1938.

The Battle of Waterloo Road. Text by Diana Forbes-Robertson. Photographs by Robert Capa. New York: Random House, 1941.

Invasion! Text by Charles C. Wertenbaker. Photographs by Robert Capa. New York: Appleton, Century, 1944.

Slightly Out of Focus. Text and photographs by Robert Capa. New York: Henry Holt, 1947.

A Russian Journal. Text by John Steinbeck. Photographs by Robert Capa. New York: Viking, 1948.

Report on Israel. Text by Irwin Shaw. Photographs by Robert Capa. New York: Simon and Schuster, 1950.

BOOKS ABOUT ROBERT CAPA

Images of War. Photographs by Robert Capa, with text from his own writings. New York: Grossman, 1964.

Robert Capa. Edited by Cornell Capa and Bhupendra Karia. (ICP Library of Photographers.) New York: Grossman, 1974.

Robert Capa: A Biography. Richard Whelan. New York: Alfred A. Knopf, 1985. Lincoln: University of Nebraska Press, 1994.

Robert Capa: Photographs. Edited by Cornell Capa and Richard Whelan. New York: Alfred A. Knopf, 1985.

Children of War, Children of Peace: Photographs by Robert Capa. Edited by Cornell Capa and Richard Whelan. Boston: Bulfinch Press/Little, Brown, 1991.

Robert Capa: Photographs. Edited by Cornell Capa, Richard Whelan, and Yolanda Cuomo. New York: Aperture, 1996.

Heart of Spain: Robert Capa's Photographs of the Spanish Civil War. Essays by Catherine Coleman, Juan P. Fusi Aizpúrua, and Richard Whelan. New York: Aperture, 1999.

A NOTE ON THE TYPE

The principal text of this Modern Library edition
was set in a digitized version of Janson,
a typeface that dates from about 1690 and was cut by Nicholas Kis,
a Hungarian working in Amsterdam. The original matrices have
survived and are held by the Stempel foundry in Germany.
Hermann Zapf redesigned some of the weights and sizes for Stempel,
basing his revisions on the original design.